Personal
Development
GOD'S WAY

BOOKS BY DOUG ADDISON

Compendium—Amazed by the Power of God Vol. 1

AVAILABLE FROM DESTINY IMAGE PUBLISHERS

Personal Development
GOD'S WAY

Doug Addison

DESTINY IMAGE® PUBLISHERS, INC.

P.O. Box 310, Shippensburg, PA 17257-0310

"Speaking to the Purposes of God for This Generation and for the Generations to Come."

This book and all other Destiny Image, Revival Press, MercyPlace, Fresh Bread, Destiny Image Fiction, and Treasure House books are available at Christian bookstores and distributors worldwide.

For a U.S. bookstore nearest you, call 1-800-722-6774.

For more information on foreign distributors, call 717-532-3040.

Reach us on the Internet: www.destinyimage.com.

Trade Paper ISBN 13: 978-0-7684-3194-0

Hardcover ISBN 13: 978-0-7684-3409-5

Large Print ISBN 13: 978-0-7684-3410-1

Ebook ISBN 13: 978-0-7684-9380-1

For Worldwide Distribution, Printed in the U.S.A.

1 2 3 4 5 6 7 8 9 10 11 / 13 12 11 10

Endorsements

God wants all His children blessed, enjoying fullness of life in His presence and goodness. In *Personal Development God's Way*, Doug Addison teaches you how to walk with God and explore His potential and divine appointed purposes for your life. A great read!

PATRICIA KING
www.XPmedia.com

Doug Addison takes a fresh, compelling approach to the unfolding of one's God-intended destiny and provides both insights and practical grounding tools from Scripture to invite us to embrace what I often refer to as God's grand design. This isn't simply a one-time read. This is a life-long learning manual for staying in step with God, staying in step with destiny, and staying in step with those God has invited to join you on the path. My thanks to Doug for making this significant investment in all of our lives.

DR. MARK J. CHIRONNA
www.markchironna.com

Doug Addison's new book on destiny is a gift at a time when encouragement is needed in a strong way in the church. We need to find ways of building ourselves and one another up as the scriptures encourage. This book is all about taking steps in obedience to understand our unique calling in Christ, thus being built up. It feels so good to walk in the strength God provides through encouragement that is rightly understood.

STEVE SJOGREN
www.ServeCoach.com

The world is crying out for tools and keys of how to live a successful and purposeful life. Many books have tried to answer those questions. But most are missing the most important element that brings that personal fulfillment. *Personal Development God's Way* by Doug Addison addresses the tension of taking charge of your destiny and having it fueled and guided by the Holy Spirit. This book will motivate the believer who has been waiting for the direction of the Lord. God has given us authority to pursue our destiny and is longing to partner with a people who are courageous and confident to go after it.

BILL JOHNSON
Bethel Church, Redding, California
Author—*When Heaven Invades Earth*
and *Face to Face With God*

I have known Doug for many years and highly recommend both the man and his message. In his honest and endearing style, Doug consistently puts to paper insightful nuggets of truth that come from his extraordinary life journey. This book is no exception and is filled with timeless and powerful concepts that will inspire your heart and revolutionize your life. In fact, the topics covered in these pages are not only rich in revelation, but are vital to the fulfillment of your God-breathed destiny. Read, enjoy, and learn from a seasoned man who is a friend of God.

LARRY RANDOLPH

Contents

Foreword

My Uncle Arnold, who was in full-time vocational ministry for over 60 years, said something to me a long time ago that stuck with me. This old-time Methodist minister said, "If you aim at nothing, you will hit it!" One time the Holy Spirit said it directly to me in another way, "You'll never hit anything you do not aim at!" That left me musing for a while!

Could that principle be true about our individual lives? We know it is true about businesses and large organizations.... But could this be true about our personal lives as well? I have never been one that did well with a Franklin planner. Some people's lives and some church ministries are so well greased, programmed, and organized, that they come off plastic. Sometimes I am amazed at how well they do with so little of God!

It is like the analogy stated by A.W. Tozer, the fabled revivalist of many years ago is said to have given: "If the Holy Spirit were removed from the church of the Book of Acts, 95 percent of what they did would cease and only 5 percent would remain. But if the Holy Spirit were removed from today's church, only 5 percent of what they do would cease and 95 percent of it would continue." Sad statement then, but it contains a truth for us today as well.

EVERY RIVER NEEDS A BANK!

There is another side to this truth as well though. In today's catch the fire, catch the Spirit, catch the next wave emphasis, sometimes we appear to be so desperate for the "current flow" that we do not have a clue where we are going! So many people and ministries go with this modus operandi because they have an identity crisis. We have to go on to something else—because God knows we sure aren't getting anywhere doing what we are! Oh my! (Some of you are not expecting to hear such comments from me!)

You see, there have to be two banks for every river! Otherwise, it might just end up being a good ride and then later you just have a bunch of runoff water to deal with. Sound familiar?

Well, I have a novel idea! Why not have both? Why not discern what the Spirit is saying in our day, our lives, our ministries, our generation, and then with His help have a plan to fulfill that calling, destiny, or purpose! Yes, let's have banks for the river and channel the waters of His presence and power into purpose and destiny with flexible plans that always yield to His will.

THE DISTINCTION OF THIS BOOK

That is where this book comes in. Doug Addison knows the realm of the Holy Spirit like few others. He is a veteran of the moves of God, and he himself is a true Spirit bearer. But he dares to bring us life-coaching practical skills to help us fulfill our dreams.

Doug challenges us to have a deeper relationship with God that embraces the power of spiritual principles that most Christians know about, but few actually practice consistently. His teachings take us into the wisdom of considering God's timing and will for your life as opposed to just going after whatever you think you might want. How refreshing!

RESULTS YOU MIGHT RECEIVE FROM THIS BOOK

- Understand more clearly what the Bible says about your personal development.

- Learn life-changing biblical principles that set you up to succeed in all areas of life.

- Uncover clues in your life about your purpose and destiny and what you have a passion for.

- Keep the past from negatively affecting your future.

- Practically renew and transform your thinking.

- Identify and change hidden ungodly beliefs and turn them into empowering new values and habits.

- Develop helpful principles for living a healthy and balanced life.

- Learn how to live a "break-through" lifestyle where all things are truly possible. Develop a life strategy with steps toward what to do next.

Wow! That makes me want to put into practice already what is in the pages of this book! So take and eat. Yes. Consume these pages and become them! Get a word and become a word! Now that alone might just be enough to create a revolution!

So join Doug Addison, myself, and many others as we search to find God's will and step out in faith, fulfilling our God-given destinies!

Blessings to you!

JAMES W. GOLL

Encounters Network • Prayer Storm • Compassion Acts

Author of *The Seer, The Lost Art of Intercession, Prayer Storm, Dream Language, Empowered Prayer,* and many more.

Introduction

People everywhere want to know more about their destiny. They want to know that their life has more purpose than going to work, coming home, cooking, and hanging out watching DVDs on the weekends. There is nothing wrong with working and hanging out, but most people want more from life than just making a living and being entertained. Life was meant to be lived with purpose, and we were all designed to have passion for living.

Purpose, passion, and creativity can get lost in our busy lives. In reality, the decisions we make every day can change our lives. Yes, I know that ultimately God's love and power are what change us, but even so, we have to make a decision to receive them. We all make decisions on a daily basis. When we learn to make the right ones for the right reasons at the right time, then the quality of our life will begin to change. If we do this consistently, we will eventually begin to break through things that have held us back in the past.

Have you ever felt like something is holding you back from moving into a greater level of fulfillment or going for your life dreams? Maybe you can identify with some of these symptoms of people who need a breakthrough in their life.

- You want to do something positive but don't know exactly where to start.

- You feel stuck in your current job, relationship, or situation.

- You feel like there is something more for you to do, but you don't know the details of what it is.

- You have difficulty making decisions or you're afraid to make a wrong decision.

- You procrastinate on a regular basis, even on things that are important for you to do.

- You have given up on some dreams, or are less passionate than you once were.

- You have gifts and talents that you rarely use.

- You feel paralyzed to move forward.

- You often have negative thoughts about yourself.

- You are waiting for the perfect situation before you begin to pursue your dreams or destiny.

- You are not taking any initiative of your own, but are waiting for God to open doors of opportunity for you.

God is limitless, and what we can do through His love and power has no limits to create a better spiritual life, career, relationships, physical health, or emotional stability. I've been studying and living the radical life-changing principles found in the Bible for over 20 years. I have found that it all starts with, and flows through, a relationship with God.

Many of the popular personal development books and seminars are based on principles found in the Bible, but they remove a personal relationship with God and His power from the equation. When you combine the radical principles of change from the Bible with a relationship with God, and add to it the empowerment through the Holy Spirit, you can accelerate into your life's purpose much more quickly than you ever dreamed possible. In the process, you will discover the supernatural life that God intended for you.

This is my life story of how I went from being involved in the occult and on drugs to becoming a very successful business owner, all through the power and grace of God. Then I went on to sell my business and pursue full-time ministry, but not in the way most people do. Though I have been a pastor, I now travel all over the world helping people to transform their lives through God's unlimited power. I train people in how to hear the voice of God, understand dreams and visions, and experience the supernatural through the Holy Spirit. In the process of meeting hundreds of thousands of people, I have observed that many Christians do not know their own destiny or spiritual gifts. As a result, I wrote this book and developed a practical training seminar that is helping people everywhere.

By using the principles taught in my seminar people are losing weight, getting new jobs, finding their spiritual gifts, writing books, starting businesses, producing new art and music, to name just a few.

So what does all this have to do with finding your destiny? If you can do smaller things in life, then you will prepare yourself for the bigger life callings. Most people live a life of avoidance and procrastination, waiting for God to speak to them and drop a sign from

Heaven. In most cases, God has already given us all that we need to move forward in our destiny. Life is like a connect-the-dots drawing; all you need to do is identify and get to the next dot; then the bigger picture will begin to take shape over time.

Whether you are just starting out in life, or you already know what you want or maybe you lost your passion along the way, this book has some practical tips and tools that can help you. I am confident when I say this, because I have road tested these principles, not only in my own life, but with thousands of people over a two-year study with my seminar, *Accelerating Into Your Life's Purpose*. The results have been amazing, and we are only beginning. Just applying these principles to my own life, I lost 30 pounds, got much healthier, and gained a lot of energy. I stopped biting my finger nails, wrote two books, deepened my relationship with God, and renewed the relationships in my life. I have gotten feedback from many other people who have taken my seminar and have made radical changes in their lives as well.

You can think of me as your personal life strategy coach as you read this book. Though I cannot be there with you personally, I can tell you that if you do the simple exercises at the end of each chapter you will experience positive changes in your life. This book is packed with powerful principles from the Bible. Even if you were to only apply one of them, your life will change. My hope and prayer is that you grab hold of the fact that all things are possible for those who believe. God is the giver of good gifts, and He is a loving Father who wants to give us good things. He wants to give us the desires of our heart, and He can do this as our heart and intentions become more like His. He wants to give you a hope, a future, and not harm you but see you prosper and succeed. You are truly a new creation in Christ, and the old things no longer have power over you unless you allow them to.

Our life purpose involves radically changing and influencing the world. Life is not just about achievement, but it is all about love and relationship. A changed life is the best witness of God's love to a world in dire need. When you change the quality of your daily life, you feel better and you are more likely to love people and connect with God on a deeper level. When you change your own life, you can't help changing the lives of those around you. We must start with ourselves, because we cannot give away what we don't have within us.

I will show you how you can develop a positive kingdom mind-set, in which you realize that God's ways are radically opposite from our own and the world around us. Most people spend their energy focusing on what is wrong with a situation as opposed to God's ultimate intentions. As we focus on God's will—which is positive and brings life—then things like bad situations, sickness, and oppression no longer have power to discourage us.

I'll also help you have a breakthrough lifestyle, in which you no longer avoid things but have discovered how to take small steps on a regular basis that will result in a radical amount of change and results over time. The secret to breaking through the things that have held you back is found in what I call the SPIN Cycle, where you no longer let the past negatively affect you; you minimize your procrastination; change any negative and ungodly internal thinking; and take care of the unclear vision. Creating a breakthrough lifestyle is not difficult to do, and it does not require a high level of intelligence, but it does involve a commitment on your part.

Going after your destiny in God will require you to change and grow in many different ways. It takes time and is a process. You will not be able to do it all at once, and it will take practice to develop new good habits. It is just like sports or playing a musical instrument. You might pick it up quickly, but to get really good at it takes practice, time, and patience. You often hear of people planning their vacations and retirement, but you don't hear much talk of people planning or designing the way they want their life to be.

Everything that happens to us is a result of our decisions, which are driven by our beliefs. So our current life situation is the direct result of what we believe about God, ourselves, and what we can accomplish through His love. Most people only believe in biblical principles with their heads but not their actions. But believing is just the first step. Doing something practical will make your faith and destiny come alive.

As we pursue our life purpose, it will really help us to hear the voice of God. After all, it is God's purposes for us that we are here to fulfill. Later I will go into how to hear God and know His timing for applying what you hear. After coaching and helping thousands of people, I realized that often God will speak to us through our dreams at night, which often can point toward our life dreams. I will teach you how to recognize destiny dreams and how to respond to them.

I mentioned previously, and I'll repeat it throughout the book, that everything starts with making a decision to do something. Usually, getting started is the toughest part. You have made a decision to read this book. I want to thank you and let you know that I am honored that you would spend your valuable time with me. Time is something you'll never get back, and I will do my best not to waste it. Instead, I'll give you some really good practical tips and tools that will help guide you to the lasting change you have always longed for.

To get the most out of this program, you will want to get a journal or notebook or use a document on your computer to complete the short assignments. I also recommend that you ask a friend to read the book as well, so you have someone you can discuss the assignments with. Often our friends and family can help us recognize things in us that we might overlook. You can go to my Web site www.personaldevelopmentgodsway.com and listen to free audios and read additional articles to support you on your journey of transformation. There are also some forms with the exercises if you want to print them out instead of writing in the book. You can also join our online community and connect with other people who are pursuing their destinies. You'll find that you are not alone, and that encouraging others will help you as well.

Are you ready to start the journey? If you are ready, then let's agree together in prayer as you start.

> *Father, I ask that you would bless these wonderful friends, who I may not know but You do. You know all the needs and longings, talents and gifts that rest in them. So I pray that you would empower them through your Holy Spirit to know You better, and to love themselves and those around them. I pray that they would gain new insight and to develop the radical supernatural lifestyle that you intended for those who believe. God, bring Your power and Your presence upon them now as they start this journey. In Jesus' name. Amen.*

Chapter 1

BEYOND BELIEF

When I was 20 years old, I read the book *The Shining* by Stephen King. For nearly ten years after that I had a reoccurring nightmare of being chased by something evil, but I was not able to run. During that year, my car caught fire and a few weeks later, while I was out with my friends, a car battery exploded in my face and I had to be rushed to the hospital. I was searching for answers. I wanted to know if God really existed; I wondered what I should do for a living; and deep questions bugged me, like, "What if Hal Lindsey was right about the end of the world and are UFOs for real?"

That was 30 years ago, and I had no clue what my destiny was. Most of my life I had focused on going to work so I could pay my bills, and, if there was anything left over, I managed to have a good time. But no matter how hard I worked or played, I would eventually end up feeling empty. I had a conflict within me because, deep inside, I felt that somehow my life must have more meaning. There must be something significant for me to accomplish, but nothing seemed to be clear.

Ever since I was young, I had felt I had a deeper purpose to fulfill, but I never knew exactly what it was, let alone how to get to it. When I was five years old, I learned a big new word, *property*. I told everyone I wanted to own property and that I wanted to help people by owning a lot of businesses. When I told my family about my dream, they laughed and thought I was cute.

They did not take me seriously until, when I was in fifth grade, I started a pet casket and burial service called Ask It Casket. I convinced my classmates to invest in my company by selling drinking straws as shares of stock so I could raise capital to buy materials to build a few pet caskets. By age 11 I had invented several devices to make my life easier. The top two were my automated bed maker and the light-turner-offer. Then things in my family's life took a turn, and I experienced a lot of tragedy and loss. By age 16, I had lost my drive to do anything, except that I wanted to write a book someday that would have answers for people who were feeling as awful as I was. It was a feeling that there was something more, but I didn't know exactly how to get there on my minimum-wage job. These thoughts and feelings preoccupied me for years.

My life story might be a little more dramatic than most people's, but maybe you can identify with parts of it. The alarm clock went off each morning, and I had to force myself out of bed to go to a job each day that I had very little energy for. Oh, I was successful in what I did, but it was not fulfilling to me. As a result I was always in the wrong relationships, over my head in debt, overworked, and overeating to try to numb the pain inside. Eventually, I sank into depression, abused alcohol, and was addicted to drugs.

That was then.

After living over half my life discouraged and directionless, I began to take steps to begin to pursue this calling to business and helping people. In the process, I made some new discoveries and brought a radical amount of change in my own life, and I have been able to help thousands of others as well. It was much more than change; it was transformation.

Now I am excited to get out of bed each day. I have a greater sense of purpose. I am not just working toward a goal; I am heading full-on into my destiny. I am having so much fun that it does not feel like I am working.

Years ago I took a huge step and left my corporate job to pursue God's greater calling on my life. I am now the founder of an organization designed to help people discover their destiny and get a deeper relationship with God. I teach people how to hear the voice of God and understand the dreams they have at night. I discovered that "night dreams" can often point us toward our "life dreams." Learning to hear God can take a lot of guesswork out of pursuing our destiny and help get us there more quickly. I am also a conference speaker and life strategy coach. I have the opportunity to travel all over the world and meet lots of different people. I speak at universities, churches, conferences, and business seminars. I found out a long time ago that if learning can be made enjoyable, then people will remember what they were taught. That's why I developed my stand-up comedy style of speaking that I use at all my seminars.

I feel great, and I have energy like never before. I know I may sound like I am some kind of motivational overachieving gearhead. But I am just an everyday guy who barely got a high school diploma and has a Rod Stewart hairdo and a 1970s Starsky and Hutch black leather jacket.

I am not financially rich as I write this, but my attitude toward life and money has changed. Even if I had millions of dollars in the bank, I would not be any happier than I am right now. I know that when you and I grasp this perspective and get our lives into balance, then nothing will stop love, finances, and opportunities from continuing to flow into our lives. Money and having nice stuff is not my goal. Don't get me wrong, I am not opposed to those things, but they are not what drives me.

> **The secret to happiness really boils down to living life with a greater sense of calling and purpose.**

What really motivates me is having the freedom to do the things that God calls me to do when He calls me to them. I once had a six-figure income as a business owner in San Francisco. Since then, I have discovered a secret that most people know in their minds but few people actually live as a lifestyle.

My life purpose is to help millions of people transform their lives and discover God's love, acceptance, and power. I like to have fun, laugh, and grow as I do it! Some people look at me and think, *It's easy for you to say these things because you have it all together.* I also hear people say, "He's got it made, and it seems that things are always going his way." That is far from the truth. It has not been an easy road at all. In fact, if I listed all the tragedies and hard times over the past 30 years, you probably would not believe me. I'll save that for a depressing book I'll write someday on how to derail your destiny through disappointing stories.

Seriously, everything that I am accomplishing and experiencing today came to me because of God's grace. It's God's love and blessings that sustain me. But these good things would not have happened had I not also made wise decisions, good choices, and found ways to get myself to move forward when I felt stuck. And, most importantly, I did not give up in hard times.

An Appointment with Destiny

Maybe you have something you have felt that you want to accomplish or do in life. Whether it is to get married, have a family, go to school, get a better job, write a book, start a business, a ministry, or whatever, you can accomplish your dreams and find a greater purpose in your life. Having a satisfying life is not just achieving things, but it is also feeling happiness and fulfillment. If you do not like an aspect of your life right now, then you really can do something about it.

Most people know these things in their head but seldom do anything about it. You might say that they know what to do, but they don't do what they know. Having a great quality of life and fulfilling your dreams is not automatic, but it does not have to be difficult either. It really all boils down to making a decision to get started. After that it is as easy as taking small steps on a regular basis. The toughest part for most people, and the thing that holds most people back, is simply taking the first step. After you get going, momentum will kick in, and it becomes easier because you have developed new habits. Yes, there will be obstacles along the way, and there will be things that try to sidetrack or set you back.

Later on, I will give you some practical tools and strategies that will help you break through your fears, frustrations, and hidden beliefs that may try to knock you down later, and I will give you ways to overcome the hardest part of not knowing where to start.

I don't know your story or how you came to read this book, but I don't believe in coincidences. There are no accidents. This is a divine connection that could possibly change your life forever. I realize that there are many different types of people with all kinds of backgrounds and stories. Your story is unique and contains its share of ups and downs and miracles as well.

I've found that perspective is everything. How you look at situations can literally make or break you. When things don't seem to be going right, you can either see it as an obstacle and be tempted to quit, or you can use it as an opportunity to grow. I wish I had developed this ability earlier in my life. I used to be very negative and had a dim outlook on life. I wondered why bad things always happened to me. I can see now that most of those bad things were not only the result of my own poor decisions but they also prepared me for what I do now. Although I would not want to repeat them, I have learned valuable life lessons in the process. I've also made some changes to stop the bad things before they happen.

An example of this is that I used to avoid things that I did not like or want to do. I had great excuses for it at the time, but it developed a habit of avoidance in my life. The result was that I was always doing things at the very last minute, which actually created more stress in my life. Since I did this in all the areas of my life, I always had a feeling of being "hit by a train" of stress and panic and did not know why. Since I have changed this behavior I can enjoy a more peaceful and stable life and still get a lot done at the same time.

Maybe you have heard all this before and you are wondering if this is just another rehashed motivational rah-rah talk. What sets what I am saying apart from the thousands of self-help and personal development books out there is the very thing that makes all the difference in life. It is developing a personal relationship with God, tapping into the power of His Holy Spirit, and applying some radical, life-changing principles found in the Bible.

It is not my intention to preach to you or try to tell you what to believe about God. You can get your hand off your wallet because I am not going to take an offering or do an altar call at the end, either. There are many views of what it means to be a Christian. Just in case you are wondering where I am coming from, I'll tell you my views up front. I see God as a positive, loving Father. He's not out to nuke us, and has lots of grace and love when we mess up. I relate with God through His Son Jesus in conjunction with the power given to us through the Holy Spirit.

I am aware of the fact that your experience and relationship with God may be different. I want you to know that I appreciate where you are right now. God knows your life better than I do. My prayer is that my stories and experiences will help and possibly motivate you in some way to move you toward a life of total fulfillment. I hope that at the end of your life on earth, you will be able to look back and be grateful and not regretful. When we get to heaven, we all want to hear those words, "Well done good and faithful servant!"

MORE THAN MOTIVATION

One of the things that I do that I enjoy the most is being a motivational speaker. This is because making positive changes in our lives requires us to get motivated in some way. Sometimes motivation comes from getting excited about something, but most of the time it is generated by being so frustrated with your current situation that you can't take it any longer. Maybe you are already pursuing your destiny, and you know the things you need to do, but are having trouble following through with them. My objective is to give you some tools that you can use to help you on your journey. If you can learn just one thing from this book that will better your life, then reading it will not be a waste of your time.

For years, I tried to find ways to get myself to do the things I thought I needed to do to change. I listened to sermons and preaching audios to improve my spiritual life, but, unfortunately, they did not influence my needed career growth or help me to find my true destiny in business. So I tried some motivational books and audios and went to personal development seminars, still trying to transform my life. I learned a lot of great things, and some of them have even changed the quality of my life. But I always went away from those events feeling like there is more to life than achieving goals and having more stuff.

Interestingly, most of the principles of change that are taught in many personal development and motivational seminars are taken *directly from the Bible*. These principles will work to change the quality of your life whether or not you are a Christian because they were designed by God. What I found out later is that if you apply them to your life in the context of a relationship with God, then you will not only have a better quality of life, you will tap into God's limitless power that will transform your life forever.

As I mentioned previously, all the good things that are happening in my life are the direct result of God's grace and love and the choices I made to respond to Him. When it comes to pursuing our destiny, what most people don't realize is that we actually can work hand in hand with God to accomplish His will. Many Christians are so afraid that they will do something that is not God's will that they often don't do anything at all. Then the pendulum swings to the other side to a group of people who are doing things that are their own desires and not what God wants for them. There is a necessary balance that requires taking some risks, and knowing when to wait on God's timing. Making mistakes and learning in the process are sometimes essential steps in moving forward in destiny. Like I said, God has lots of grace for us, especially when we are learning.

Keep in mind a *very powerful principle* that you are probably already aware of:

> *But seek first His kingdom and His righteousness, and all these things will be given to you as well* (Matthew 6:33).

If you place a high value on your spiritual life and on building a relationship with God, then He will guide you through all areas of your life. I can't tell you how many times I have gotten so busy doing things *for* God that I forfeited spending time *with* Him. Then I started spending so much time reading, studying, and praying that I neglected to help other people or to pursue my destiny. We definitely need a balance!

BEYOND BELIEVING

As a Christian, I often hear people say that happiness and fulfillment come only from a relationship with Jesus. This statement is true, and I have experienced it in my life, for sure. But after being around Christianity for a while, I had some questions.

Why are there so many Christians who seem just as unhappy and unfulfilled as people who do not have a relationship with God? And, if God loves everyone the same, then why do some Christians seem to be more blessed by God than others? This baffled me because we all serve the same God—right? Why are so many Christians over their heads in debt, divorced, overweight, depressed, and clueless about their destiny? I don't mean to be judgmental toward anyone who has any of these problems. I am just thinking out loud about these obvious contradictions.

It is true that you can believe and receive God's love and acceptance because God will freely give it to you if you simply ask. *The principle of believing and receiving is necessary, and our faith is built on it.* When it comes to God's love, you don't have to do anything to prove yourself. All you have to do is believe and receive:

> *Yet to all who received him, to those who believed in his name, he gave the right to become children of God* (John 1:12).

What most people miss is that believing is just the first step into a new life. There is more for us to do to experience a radically transformed life. I have always thought that there has to be something missing. This is what drove me to find out why some Christians have a great quality of life and others do not. Some seem to be truly fulfilled and are shining examples of a radical new life!

I have noticed that people who seem to be blessed more than others are quite clear in what they believe, and they are proactive about it. They are always doing things that make their faith real and practical. They invite people to their house, give to people in need, take time to listen to someone's problems, and they help connect people to solutions. They are always giving to others, and yet they have their own needs met and more. Then I realized one day that Jesus laid it out for us quite clearly in this spiritual principle:

> *Jesus said, "Ask and it will be given to you; seek and you will find; knock and the door will be opened to you* (Matthew 7:7).

Notice that the words *ask, seek,* and *knock* are all proactive steps. They also are an acronym A.S.K. Jesus did not say, "Believe and the door will be opened." Or even, "Sit on the couch and wait for God to open the door." Again, there is power in believing and power in waiting on God. But to cash in on all that God has for you requires taking steps and being proactive.

There are many other similar principles in the Bible that are keys that will unlock and open the door to your future. They will also close doors to negative things from your past. The problem is that most Christians only believe these principles in their minds and have not practiced them consistently in their daily lives. When we do them we will start to see the radical transformation of a new life.

Believing and then doing something practical in response is necessary to pursue your destiny in God. It will take an intentional effort on your part to find and fulfill your life destiny through God's strength and power. It starts with believing and receiving all that God has for you.

> *If you believe, you will receive whatever you ask for in prayer* (Matthew 21:22).

I have heard so many great testimonies from people who have grasped this principle for the first time in their lives. One of my favorites is a young woman named Erin. She grew up in a Christian home, believing that if you just have faith, God will take care of the rest. Though it is a true statement, somehow she got to a place where she found herself waiting on God to do things for her. She needed a new car but did not have a down payment to buy one, so she prayed and waited a year, but her situation did not change. She was at a church where I spoke on taking proactive steps and working hand in hand with God. The light went on, and she began asking advice and found a very creative way to cut her budget and save money. Someone told her to sell her current car and then act like she had already bought the car and to begin placing her future car payment into her savings now. She had to borrow rides for a while, but within three months she was able to buy the car she wanted!

Sometimes spiritual people get too spiritually minded and avoid actually doing something practical. Being proactive allows you to try new things, make a plan, and let God guide you through the steps to get there.

> *In his heart a man plans his course, but the Lord deter-mines his steps* (Proverbs 16:9).

Many times I have thought something was going to go one way, and it turned out completely differently. God guides us through because quite often it is the process of pursuing something that teaches us the necessary lessons that we need to grow and mature. As I look back, I can see that God guided me even through my mistakes.

IT'S NEVER TOO LATE

Everything that I am sharing with you I have actually done myself and continue to do on a regular basis. I have spent well over 1,500 hours researching and developing the message in this book. I am not speaking from theory, but coaching you from experience.

After studying and living these powerful principles for over 20 years, a few years ago I had allowed myself to sink again into a state of despair and feeling overwhelmed. Even though I knew what I needed to do, I found myself caught up in trying to do things without having a clear focus or plan. As a result, I was out of shape, overweight, stressed out, overworked, and I had lost my peace with God.

One day I could not take it any longer, so I decided to put into action what I already know how to do. We had just moved to Los Angeles to start a new ministry, and I was developing new courses on creative new ways to share God's love that were helping thousands of people at my seminars. I was exhausted from traveling and working all the time, and I started believing a lie that I did not have enough time to do anything about changing my situation. My only solution was to work more, and it got me more discouraged.

Maybe you can identify with some of the areas of my life that I needed to change. I wanted to be a living example of God's transforming power and have more energy, so I needed to work on my physical body so that I could live longer and be healthy and accomplish all that God has destined for me to do.

I was told by many people that I should write a book on prophetic evangelism so that I could go from helping thousands of people to impacting millions around the world without having to travel so much. I wanted to have more money so that we could give to causes that my wife and I value, and have the freedom to do what God calls me to do without having to work so hard all the time. We wanted to get out of debt and buy a house, develop a retirement plan, and leave an inheritance to my family.

Most of all, I wanted to have peace so that I could hear the voice of God and have time to study all that God was showing me at that time. I knew the principle of "seek first the Kingdom of God," so a deeper relationship with God was essential. I knew that I would have to find a way to slow down and gain more peace in my life. We were launching a new ministry and starting a new church at the same time. We did not have much cash flow and were not able to hire a staff. Consequently, we did a lot of the work ourselves.

Here's what happened when I applied the principles in this book. In a matter of three weeks, I was able to gain so much peace that I stopped biting my fingernails for the first time in my life! That was a big deal for me. I began spending time in prayer and study, and God showed me what to strategically focus on at any given time to maximize my impact with a minimal amount of time and effort.

I started exercising regularly, lost 30 pounds, and have kept it off for over six years. I went down four pant sizes and two shirt sizes. I'm now at my ideal weight for my body size, as skinny as I am. Some people are big boned; well, I'm small boned.

In those three weeks, I was able to write the initial manuscript for a book that I had been trying to write for three years. Before I was drinking six shots of espresso a day just to stay alert. When I stopped drinking coffee at that level, I nearly bankrupted Starbucks.

Now, I feel better and have more energy than ever. I'm not saying you have to give up coffee, but there are healthy ways to get energy that don't crash you afterward. By the way, I'm now a social coffee drinker, only on occasion or for fun.

When I started my ministry, my wife and I were literally working from 9 A.M. to 11 P.M. in our office that was in our townhouse. We had tried on several occasions to hire a staff to help us, but simply could not afford it. There was still too much work for the two of us, but we could not get the help we needed to grow.

Here's what happened after steadily living these principles of change. In less than a year we had five employees and an office with an ocean view in Santa Monica, California. A year later, we bought a house that resulted in a financial blessing during the economic downturn in the United States because we were able to sell that house and buy another one, and with intentional changes in our spending it has resulted in our being debt free except for our house.

> **When you find out what motivates you, then you can move from just working and making a living to living a life of meaning and fulfillment.**

All this is fun and great, but as I said before, it is not what I live for. I am motivated by helping others. When you find out what motivates you, then you can move from just working and making a living to living a life of meaning and fulfillment. To get myself out of despair, I had to get intentional about pursuing my dreams and life destiny again. I had to make a plan and follow through, or none of what I am experiencing today would be happening. It was definitely not my own strength or wisdom that made these things happen. Even though I had a plan, God stepped in on several occasions and surprised us by giving us new opportunities. Because I had been pro-active all along, I was ready and alert when God put the opportunities there for us to pursue.

There are millions of people who have a destiny to be world changers. Most of them have the experience, training, talents, and gifts to do it. What they lack is simply the ability to make a plan, break through their fears, and follow through.

I hear a lot of Christians say that they don't need goals or a plan because they trust God and follow the Spirit. Well, Jesus had a goal to go to Jerusalem and die on a cross. Paul had a goal to go to Rome and witness to Caesar. I'd say it is okay to have goals, especially if God is directing you. Knowing what you want to accomplish helps you get clear on what you will need and how to stay on track.

It is never too late to start. Ever hear of the painter "Grandma" Moses? She didn't start painting until she was in her seventies. She was self-taught, a widow and mother of ten (only five of whom survived infancy); Grandma Moses became an American celebrity. She was one of the most famous American folk artists of the twentieth century.

EXERCISE: WHAT ARE YOU PUTTING OFF?

One of the most difficult things about changing your life is simply getting started. Once you take the first step, you start to see how easy it is, you develop momentum, and eventually it will become a new good habit. Making a decision to act is what will change your life. You will move from just believing it is a good thing—to actually doing it. This is what separates those who obtain what they want from the ones who just talk about it.

1. Make a decision.
   What one or two decisions or tasks have you been putting off that if you did them would change your life in some way? Maybe you want to take steps to get out of debt, lose weight, reconcile a broken relationship, clean up your office, or find out more about going to college or on a ministry trip? Write two of them down.

2. Do something.
   What are one or two simple steps you can do today that will help you with your new decision? Do you need to write a letter or e-mail to someone? Make a phone call? Purchase a book, DVD, or organizer? Do some research on the Internet about it? Take a class? Make sure you are specific and follow through by doing it right now or sometime today.

You can go to www.personaldevelopmentgodsway.com to download the exercise so that you can do it on your computer.

Chapter 2

A JOURNEY TO DISCOVER CHANGE

NEW DISCOVERIES

Let me tell you more about how I made these discoveries that radically transformed my life. Looking back on my experiences, I can see why I was able to suddenly bring the changes I needed after failing so many times in the past. Like many people, I had ups and downs in my life. I had tried Christianity several times before, but nothing seemed to work to bring lasting, long-term change.

In my late twenties I had a radical encounter with Jesus that rocked my world. To make a long story short, when I first came to Jesus for the second time I was 19, I had been born again and again and again, but after a year or so I would divert back to my old ways. So in my twenties, I ended up back on drugs and involved in the occult and was pretty hopeless. My sister, who had become a Christian, had been praying for me, and she told me that I had destiny to do something really great for God. Early one morning she called me and said that

Jesus had told her He would remove the evil spirits that were holding me back if I would ask Him to do it. I mumbled a short prayer later that day, and one week later, all the heaviness and darkness lifted off me as I was driving to work.

I remember very clearly that I was set free and was so grateful. I rededicated my life to Jesus and got involved with a great church that helped me to grow in my spiritual gifts and get the emotional healing I needed to stick with it. It truly was a transformational time of my life. Though there were still some difficult times, I discovered a new strength and power through the Holy Spirit that helped me through. It was a combination of God's love and power and some new relationships with people who cared for me that made the difference.

I also made another new discovery at the same time in my life. I didn't realize this at the time, but things began to fall together like pieces to a puzzle. I had been praying for a better job, and immediately I got a great new job in San Francisco that was a step up for me to move up into middle management. This gave me confidence that I could actually make something of my life. Then something miraculous happened. The company I was working for sent me to management and personal development training designed for executive-level management and officers for companies and large corporations. The president of my company was not able to attend this training, and they were going to lose their money. As God would have it, no one else was able to go, so they sent me, a supervisor of the credit department. Yes, I was sharing God's love as a bill collector!

The training was very cutting-edge in the 1980s and cost my employer several thousand dollars. When I arrived, I was surprised that all of the other attendees were executive managers from influential companies in the San Francisco Bay area. They chuckled at my passion and drive despite my young age and lack of education and experience. I felt awkward but gave it my all.

I spent five days learning a lot about who I am and what drives me to do the things that I do. I began to understand my personality style and how to do tasks in ways that keep me challenged and motivated and how to avoid the things that bog me down. I also learned about goal setting and developed a career plan with easy steps that I could do right away to make it practical. I began moving toward making many dreams in my life a reality. For the first time I felt like I was truly alive. I had peace with God, and I was growing spiritually. I had a great job, and now I had some practical tools to go along with my faith to change my life.

It was not the training alone that changed me. It was God's love and power in my life combined with learning to make good choices and taking steps to change. I noticed that when I applied these principles to other areas of my life I was able to bring radical changes there as well. My spiritual life deepened, my emotional condition stabilized, I began having better relationships, and I experienced a financial increase.

I didn't know why it was working, but it was working, and I loved it. My career skyrocketed! Suddenly, I was employee of the year, and I got 11 of the 13 performance awards that year at work. I bought a brand-new truck and a new house. This was just a couple of years after I had been so hopeless that I had considered ending my life. I was promoted from a supervisor to the manager of several departments.

My relationships changed dramatically when I stopped hanging around people who had a negative influence on me. I began to experience a balance emotionally because I was learning to make better decisions and dramatically decreased doing things that were not good for me. Spiritually, I began to grow and mature and was now part of the leadership at my church. At first, I kind of felt guilty about all the change I was experiencing because many of my Christian friends seemed to be stuck in their lives and could not find their purpose. I always kept a perspective that it was God who brought these new opportunities into my life as a result of my relationship with Him.

One day the thought came to me that if we could only take some of the things that I learned in the management training and apply them to what is being taught in churches, then we would see a massive amount of change in people everywhere. One of my primary spiritual gifts was evangelism. I knew that a changed life is the best witness of God's power, so this could be a huge key to help reach people with God's love.

I was excited about these new possiblities, so I talked about it with my pastor and other Christian friends. They thought I was nuts. They wondered if I was involved in some kind of "Kool-Aid drinking cult." As I studied it deeper, I realized that most of the principles being taught in these seminars are actually principles from the Bible. So why are business seminars teaching principles from the Bible that work to change people's lives and most churches are not? It was beyond me, but all of this was two decades ago.

Since that time, I have grown in my spiritual life and have discovered my life purpose and destiny. Several years ago God directed me to gather these radical biblical principles of change and help people get unstuck and fulfill their life's purpose by building a relationship with Him and utilizing the power of His Holy Spirit. It doesn't get any better than that!

THIS IS NOT POSITIVE THINKING

Now that you have heard my story, you might think that I am talking about the power of positive thinking or positive speaking. I have been accused by some for bringing New Age theology into the Church, which is far from the truth. Let me show you the difference.

There is a huge movement going on all around the world called the personal development or human potential movement. It sprang up in the 1960s and encompassed a wide array of positive thinkers, motivational gurus, and New Age therapeutic healers. I want to be very clear that I am *not* teaching from this standpoint. Although at times there are things I will mention that may sound similar to those teachings, it is because they actually borrowed many of their concepts from the Bible, but they remove a personal relationship with God from the equation. This allows their teachings to sound somewhat biblical, but their theology is humanistic.

The positive thinkers say that all you have to do is think positive thoughts, and eventually you will become and receive what you think if you do it consistently. There are elements of truth in that statement, but there is a flaw as well. The danger to this way of thinking is that whatever we pursue must be in God's will and timing. You can think or say over and over, "I am a movie star, I am a movie star," but it will not make you a movie star unless you find ways to get practical training and develop yourself in this area. You can begin to focus intently on something you want, and one way or another you will find a way to get it. Again, whatever we go after must be in God's will and timing.

Let's look at this deeper. The Bible does teach the value of thinking positively and transforming your mind. Here is a good example:

> *Do not conform any longer to the pattern of this world,*
> *but be transformed by the renewing of your mind. Then*
> *you will be able to test and approve what God's will*
> *is—his good, pleasing and perfect will* (Romans 12:2).

The apostle Paul talked quite a bit about renewing your mind and thinking and meditating on good and positive things:

> *Finally, brothers, whatever is true, whatever is noble, whatever is right, whatever is pure, whatever is lovely, whatever is admirable—if anything is excellent or praiseworthy—think about such things.* (Philippians 4:8 TNIV).

Thinking positively is a very good practice and is a necessary step toward transforming and renewing your mind. Since "Positive Thinking" is now a coined phrase that is associated with a New Age type of movement, I like to refer to it as "thinking positively," which is very biblical and not New Age if you renew your mind through God's love and power through the Holy Spirit. I will unpack my theory more later on.

Os Hillman has great insight into this subject in his article, *The Error in Positive Thinking*:

> God's people should be the most positive, joyful people on earth. This joy should be a by-product of a healthy, intimate relationship with Jesus. In today's business climate, we are barraged with every possible means of becoming more productive workplace believers. Positive thinking and self-help philosophy are promoted as tools for workplace believers to fulfill their potential and overcome the mountains in their lives. God calls each of us to be visionary leaders, but we must be careful that vision is born out of His Spirit, not the latest self-help program. These ideas lead us away from dependence on God to a self-based psychology designed to give us more power, prosperity, and significance.
>
> The result is heresy. Our faith in God becomes faith in faith. It is born out of hard work and diligence rather than obedience to God is Spirit. The problem lies in that these philosophies sound good, and can even be supported by

Bible verses. Beware of anything that puts the burden of performance on you rather than God. There are times in our lives when God doesn't want us to climb every mountain. Sometimes He wants us to go around. Knowing the difference is the key to being a man or woman led by the Spirit.

God has called us to affect the workplace through His Spirit, not by our might. Have you tapped into the real power source of the soul? Ask the Lord to reveal and empower you through His Spirit today. Then you will know what real positive thinking is.[1]

THE SECRET BEHIND THE SECRET

A youth leader from a church approached me about the DVD, *The Secret.* She had been showing it to the youth at her church, and they were beginning to see amazing answers to their prayer requests. She asked me if it was OK to be doing this; after all, it was encouraging the youth to pray. That conversation prompted me to include the following section in this book.

Maybe you have heard about the "The Law of Attraction." It was made popular in 2007 by the book and DVD, *The Secret* by Rhonda Byrne. Byrne and many other New Age and positive thinking motivational gurus claim that we can actually create what we want simply by thinking it and asking for it. It is controversial in the science world because their hypothesis defies current understanding of scientific principles. They do, however, have an amazing number of testimonies that it does work.

If you are a Christian and you are practicing the Law of Attraction or you know someone who is, please consider what I have to say. If you are not a Christian and you practice this, then please understand that

43

I am not judging you. If you are seeking the truth, eventually you will stumble upon God who can offer an incredible amount of fulfillment, peace, and joy to your life. My intent is to help shed some light on the subject, bring it into perspective, and provide an alternative to the process.

Though the actual steps in the Law of Attraction taught by the self-help and Positive Thinking experts vary based on what book you read, most of the positive thinking gurus teach people to follow these steps:

- You must be certain as to what it is you want.

- Then ask the Universe to give it to you.

- On a regular basis, begin to visualize yourself receiving it, holding it, experiencing what it is you want.

- Be open to the fact that your answer may come in any form.

You may recognize many biblical principles in these steps:

Therefore I tell you, whatever you ask for in prayer, believe that you have received it, and it will be yours (Mark 11:24).

Now faith is being sure of what we hope for and certain of what we do not see (Hebrews 11:1).

...He (Abraham) is our father in the sight of God, in whom he believed, the God who gives life to the dead and calls things that are not as though they were (Romans 4:17).

There are elements of truth to the Law of Attraction. My concern is the motivation behind it. We do need to be clear on what it is we want in life, and we need to ask God to fulfill it. The major difference between the Law of Attraction and the message of the Bible is that when you ask for something, you should ask God directly in the context of a personal relationship, as opposed to a cosmic "Universe" force that is somewhere out there. When we ask, we need to believe that He hears us and will answer our prayer one way or another. We do need to be cautious not to visualize something to the point that we are meditating on the item itself that we are asking for. This could easily cross over into idolatry. Remember, it is God who is the giver and the source of all good gifts.

> *Don't be deceived, my dear brothers. Every good and perfect gift is from above, coming down from the Father of the heavenly lights, who does not change like shifting shadows* (James 1:16-17).

Even though there are elements of truth in the claim of *The Secret*, they are very clear that they are *not* talking about asking the God of the Bible. They view God as a positive energy or force and not as a person. If you practice the Law of Attraction, be sure not to remove the source of true life and renewed thinking, which is the Holy Spirit and the God of the Bible. The very people who took these biblical principles out of context and developed this humanistic teaching are in danger of being blind to the greater truth. They might be tapping into God's principles, but they are not tapping into God's love and power.

DOING IT GOD'S WAY

God created the world by speaking it into being. You are created in His image; therefore, you too have a creative power to speak into situations and bring about radical change. One of the missing elements of the Law of Attraction is the principle I mentioned previously of seeking God first. You need to be sure that what you are asking for is in His will and timing for your life. This balance is the powerful spiritual principle that will allow all the things you need to flow to you, instead of you trying to visualize them and trying to get them to come your way.

> *But seek first his kingdom and his righteousness, and all these things will be given to you as well* (Matthew 6:33).

I am not recommending at all that you read the book or watch *The Secret*. But if you have, or you are practicing the Law of Attraction, I hope you can see the points that I am making here and can receive this word of wisdom. You can safely tap into God's powerful biblical principles by doing the following steps:

- Develop a relationship with God through Jesus Christ and spend time regularly with Him in prayer and study. It will be out of this relationship with God that your prayers will be answered. Learn to recognize the voice of God when He is speaking to you.

- Ask God to show you that what you are asking for is something that He wants you to have or do. Ask for wisdom and for His timing.

- Once you determine that what you want is within the context of God's will for your life, then have faith and believe that God will answer you. One way or another, He will answer your prayers.

- Pray and ask God for the things that you want and need. Be sure to track them and watch for answered prayer to strengthen your faith.

- Be prepared for the answer to come in a variety of ways. The answers to your prayers may look different than you expect when you get an answer to prayer, let others know so that they can give God glory with you.

- Share your success stories with others so that their faith will be strengthened and they can receive encouragement.

God wants only the best for us all. He wants us to live our lives to our fullest potential. These radical principles of change have always been in the Bible, but unfortunately in our day and age it was not a Christian who pointed them out to the world. Most people are running their spiritual tanks on empty and many are at only half-throttle compared to what God has in mind for them. God's love and power is limitless. The only thing that limits us is what we think we can actually accomplish and what we believe about God.

Over the past 20 years, I have developed what I call a *breakthrough lifestyle* that is actually similar to the Law of Attraction. It is based on Matthew 7:7 in which Jesus told us to "ask, seek, and knock," and we will receive. I have actively applied many of the life-changing principles from the Bible and have obtained some radical results. Even more importantly, I have done it all in the context of a personal relationship with God through Jesus. I will get into this concept more later on.

A friend of mine, Jamie, got a hold of what I was saying about developing a lifestyle of breaking through. She started exercising and lost 15 pounds within a short time. She was so encouraged that she began to pursue a music project that she had set aside. Within three months, she finished the project and produced her own CD and is selling it on iTunes.

GOD'S WILL AND TIMING

One thing that can limit us in pursuit of our destiny is what we think we can actually accomplish. I realize that this can be a dangerous message. On one hand, you need to be careful not to focus on your own strength to bring the changes into your life. God must be your source of strength and energy. On the other hand, you must take action, be proactive, and move forward, or you will run the risk of getting stagnant and stuck.

An often-difficult part of finding your destiny is to know what to focus on at any given time. Here are three examples of understanding God's timing. First, there may be periods of time in your life that God is teaching you lessons to grow deeper to spiritual maturity. It may seem as though He is holding you back, but in reality He is training you. It is important to recognize these times so that you can work with God and not strive to accomplish something that is not time for you to do yet. Second, it helps to be aware of times when God is testing you and wants you to move forward. Third, spiritual warfare you are pursuing for the next steps God has for you and you are on target, but dark forces try to hold you back. So knowing what is happening with timing is very crucial.

The point I am trying to make is that you cannot just go out full-on to try to get whatever you want and assume it is God's will for your life. Your destiny will unfold over time, and it will happen in God's timing. Be sure, though, that you are holding up your end of the deal by pursuing it.

I meet people all the time who are afraid to move forward because they don't want to make a mistake or get out of God's timing. If you are afraid to move forward then be aware that a negative force may be trying to hold you back by scaring you into believing that you are not in God's timing.

Getting out of these negative patterns will require change. It is similar to training for a sport or learning to play an instrument. You would not be able to do it well if you tried just a few times. It will require conditioning yourself and practice. Soon, it will become automatic and much easier.

EXERCISE: DO IT GOD'S WAY

Think for a minute about something you would like to accomplish or have in your life. Maybe you want to go into real estate; you need a new car; you want or need to go back to school; you want to attend a ministry training school, or whatever it is for you.

Decide on one thing then go through the steps listed in the section "Doing It God's Way" (page 45). Write it out and place it in your Bible or somewhere you will see it. Go through the steps and pray your request every day for at least the next two weeks or even a month.

You can go to www.personaldevelopmentgodsway.com to download the exercise so that you can do it on your computer.

ENDNOTE

1. Os Hillman, "The Error in Positive Thinking," September 17, 2006, http://www.marketplaceleaders.org/.

Chapter 3

POWER OF A POSITIVE LIFESTYLE

NEW CHRISTIAN PARKING SPACES

My early church experiences were dry and boring. I had only known about God in a factual way. I knew about the Bible and that God loved me, but I had no idea that the Christian life could be so interactive. Then I discovered that God wants us to experience His love not only in our minds but also through the supernatural power and presence of the Holy Spirit. I was so amazed at all the cool things that began to happen to me. For instance, I would pray for a parking place and "bingo," there was one right up front. Every day was a new adventure as I was learning and experiencing God in ways I'd never dreamed possible. Another time, I was telling my non-Christian friends that I had been praying for a job. The telephone literally rang right then, and it was a job! They were freaked out and ran out of the room because suddenly God became real.

I have story after story about how my faith is now alive. It was like connecting with God through high-speed Internet as opposed to dialup. There is so much more available than most people realize. Early in my journey with God, I was telling my new Christian friends at church about my experiences. They told me that God does this for all new Christians to get their attention, but later I will need to grow up and become mature. They said that when I become mature He won't have to do miracles all the time, and that I would soon be like them. The sad thing is that I believed them. Soon, I stopped experiencing God in this way and, though I grew in knowledge, I had lost track of the supernatural aspect of being a Christian.

One day I realized that God wants us all to experience Him supernaturally all the time. We do need to grow and mature and trust God, even when we don't see miracles happening daily. God wants us to have this "new Christian" experience with Him all the time. I started asking God to speak to me and provide all the fun answers and surprises I used to experience, and sure enough, they started happening again. Though not all my parking spaces are out front, I get lots of fun surprises as God speaks to me. It deepens my relationship with Him and increases my faith.

Now I pray regularly that God will be real to me today. Not just head knowledge but, "God, let me see You in practical ways." I ask Him to use me to help people along my way. I continually have "divine encounters" with people in public places.

- Right now, if you want to experience God in this way, simply ask Him to make Himself real to you. Ask Him to surprise you with something that you will know is from Him.

- Pray daily for God to speak to you about your situation and for people around you.

- Write down things that you hear God say and things you experience. Share it with other people to encourage them as well.

GOD IS LAVISH!

When I read the Bible I cannot help noticing the extravagant descriptions of God. Streets of gold, gems, brilliant light, to name a few. God owns everything, and He is a lavish God. But when I go into many different types of churches, I sense the desperation in the people, almost as though they were begging for money with a tin cup.

I'm really not being judgmental. In fact, my family roots are from the southern part of the United States, where a favorite saying is "bless their hearts," which is a free pass for you to talk about others without being accused of judging them (joke).

I soon realized that many Christians are not living their lives to the fullest potential God has in mind for them. So I studied the powerful promises, blessings, and spiritual principles that are available to us. I guess it was easy for me to see this since I once was involved in deep darkness of the occult back in the 1980s. When I came out of darkness and into God's awesome light, I was amazed at the power available to us through the Holy Spirit. I had experienced and seen many things spiritually. But once I came into God's Kingdom, I realized that what I experienced in the occult was merely a pilot light compared to God's brilliant light.

For God, who said, "Let light shine out of darkness," made his light shine in our hearts to give us the light of the knowledge of the glory of God in the face of Christ (2 Corinthians 4:6).

Since I have been on both sides of the fence, so to speak, I have a more positive perspective toward the Christian life now. All characteristics and qualities of God are positive. God is love (see 1 John 4:8), and there is nothing negative about Him. God has nothing but good intentions for us and wants us to succeed in all that we do (see Jer. 29:11-13). On the other hand, all aspects of satan are darkness and negative.

> *The thief comes only to steal, kill and destroy; I have come that they may have life, and have it to the full* (John 10:10).

GOD'S WAYS ARE OPPOSITE OF OURS

When I was involved in the occult, I recognized negative things like depression, sickness, repeated accidents, and traumatic events as being motivated from the dark realm. When I became a Christian, I saw a stark contrast between the Spirit of God and the spirit of this world. I am not trying to scare you, but to encourage you with the fact that God has so much to offer that many Christians are not aware of.

I noticed that God's ways are often opposite to what we experience in the culture and world around us. The following list of things that Jesus said illustrates how opposite to our way of thinking God's way is: that we should turn the other cheek if someone strikes us; if we are asked for something, we should give it freely; we need to bless those who curse or mistreat us; love our enemies; build up and not tear down; forgive and we will be forgiven; the first will be last; and we need to be humble to be lifted up—you get my drift.

All these teachings of Jesus are opposite of the ways of the world which are revengeful, angry, unforgiving, and self-centered. This behavior is very apparent in the popular reality television shows. We commonly hear phrases like, "You're fired; you are voted off the island; you're voted out because America does not like you." The camera often gets in the face of the person who is experiencing public humiliation and rejection and milks it even more. There is a mean spirit behind this type of entertainment. They often invite people to be on these shows who are already a little emotionally unstable, and then exploit the person's pain and weakness.

There is a different type of reality television show called the "make-over." It is actually more along the lines of God's heart for people. The encouraging and uplifting focus of the show is to build a person up through kindness and to help them in some practical way. We can learn a great lesson from this type of reality show. People really like to be encouraged and lifted up. I think we all need an *extreme makeover* in some aspect of our lives.

Since God's ways are opposite to the world's, then our behavior as Christians should reflect this. I'm not talking about just being moral, but being a bright shining example in every aspect of life. It seems that as representative of God's life-changing power, we can be examples of good health, emotional stability, financial security, and unconditional love.

I have noticed that many Christians that I meet tend to focus on negative things instead of positive things. They often look at what is wrong with a person as opposed to all the good things that God gifted them with. This causes Christians to appear to be judgmental when they may not mean to come off that way. I realize that their intentions might be good—to help people—but it can be interpreted differently by people outside of Christianity.

If you want to test my theory that Christians tend to be more negative than positive ("bless their hearts"), then go ask people at random what they think of Christians and Christianity. The overwhelming opinion is that Christians are judgmental, self-righteous, intolerant, interested in getting your money, and out of touch with the real issues of the world. I did not make these up; I actually have heard these over and over as I talk with people in my travels and doing evangelistic outreaches. These are not the characteristics we want people to know us for, and it is not the behavior of Christ or His disciples.

Please understand that I am not trying to be negative on Christians or churches. I have been a pastor, and a lot of my best friends are Christians. I am just being honest, and I would like to offer a solution to the things I mentioned above about how others see Christians. Let's take a look at how Jesus interacted with people of His day.

THE POWER OF ENCOURAGEMENT

I noticed something interesting when I started to study the way Jesus interacted with people who were not religious. First of all, Jesus only got angry at religious people, who did not love people but were ripping them off instead. Jesus was actually quite uplifting and encouraging to people.

When Jesus first met Nathanael (see John 1:45-51), He said to him, *"Here is a true Israelite, in whom there is nothing false."* Nathanael was amazed that Jesus knew this about him. Basically Jesus called him an honest man, and that small act of encouragement opened Nathanael up to receive from Jesus and become one of His disciples.

Jesus encountered the Samaritan woman at a well (see John 4:7-30, 39-41). During their conversation, Jesus told the woman a little about herself: she had been married five times and was not married to the man she now lived with. He did this without condemning her; had Jesus been judging her, He would have called her an adulterous woman. Instead, when she admitted that she had no husband, Jesus said to her, "What you said is quite honest." Jesus always looked for the positive in people. As a result, the woman's response was, "Sir, I perceive you to be a prophet." The entire town of Samaria was impacted that day.

A great example of the power of encouragement is when a woman who was caught in the act of adultery was brought before Jesus (see John 8:1-12). The custom of that day was that she be put to death. Jesus stood up for her and said the following:

> *Jesus straightened up and asked her, "Woman, where are they? Has no one condemned you?" "No one, sir," she said. "Then neither do I condemn you," Jesus declared. "Go now and leave your life of sin"* (John 8:10-11).

There are many examples of how Jesus and His disciples encouraged people and brought the positive light of God into a world of darkness. There is power in love and encouragement. We must be careful not to focus our attention too much on the negative things with others and within ourselves, but instead find the positive in everything and everyone. It is a spiritual principle that changes the spiritual atmosphere around you. People want to be with you because you are a positive influence, and they feel safe and can open up and trust you. When you do this for yourself, you will discover a deeper level of God's grace on your life.

> *Finally, brothers, whatever is true, whatever is noble, whatever is right, whatever is pure, whatever is lovely, whatever is admirable—if anything is excellent or praiseworthy—think about such things. Whatever you have learned or received or heard from me, or seen in me—put it into practice. And the God of peace will be with you* (Philippians 4:8-9).

Robert was dissatisfied with life but could not put his finger on why. He felt irritated by other people at work who did not share his religious and political views. After taking my class on the power of encouragement, he was able to see that his co-workers were people who needed what he had. He then changed his entire outlook and began to envision a greater purpose for his job. He started encouraging people and looking for the best in them. He now feels like his job is a ministry, and the dissatisfaction has long left him.

DEVELOPING A POSITIVE KINGDOM PERSPECTIVE

When we continually focus our attention on things that are wrong, negative, or that don't work, then we can start to see the world through a negative viewpoint and start believing this is the reality everywhere. Just watch the news on television and you can start thinking that things are very bad everywhere. Fear and hopelessness can set in, and we start thinking that the world is going down—so what is the use anyway? Well the true reality is that God is still in charge, and last I checked, He is still in a good mood. His love and changing power is still available to us all. We must develop what Jesus referred to as "eyes that see." We must have the belief that nothing is too difficult for God.

God's love and power are much stronger than any demonic power. We have nothing to fear. It helps to get the perspective that powers of darkness in this world are trying to destroy God's creation. We must be careful not to buy into the lie that we are all doomed. So when we see someone suffering from things like depression, suicidal thoughts, or sickness, we must realize that this is not the will of God for this person or even ourselves. It is the plan of the enemy to steal their life and destiny. Since God's love and will for us is the only true reality, we must recognize the works of darkness as a counterfeit and deterrent to God's intentions for us.

We can learn a very powerful strategy in the three encounters I just mentioned where Jesus encourages people to change their lives. When you see the works of darkness in a person's life, or your own for that matter, you have the opportunity to positively turn it around and bring God's love and encouragement which will lead to a new life.

> *"...The reason the Son of God appeared was to destroy the devil's work"* (1 John 3:8).

I am continually looking to encourage people who are suffering from negative influences. When I offer love and encouragement to others, I see the greatest changes happen in their lives. I have developed a strategy that I call "Fliptastic," or "flipping" a negative situation using a positive Kingdom perspective. It is the ability to recognize the negative things of satan, turn them around, and interject God's love and kindness into that situation. Suddenly, a light comes on where there was no hope. I see "mini miracles" all the time by simply finding something positive in a person and pointing it out to them.

First John 4:4 tells us that the Spirit within us is greater than the one in the world around us (my paraphrase). Science has discovered that there is a major difference between light and dark. Light can be measured; it has substance and mass, and when it moves it has force. Darkness, however, is the absence of light. Jesus is Light, and Paul encourages us to live as children of Light. When we do this, we bring God's presence with us everywhere we go, even if we are not aware of it. Living our lives with a greater measure of God's love and light is extremely powerful. We dispel darkness, sometimes without having to say a word, because the Spirit within us is powerful and healing.

> *For you were once darkness, but now you are light in the Lord. Live as children of light* (Ephesians 5:8).

As Christians, we need to understand and regularly practice positive spiritual principles of praying for those who curse us, loving those who hate us, giving to those in need, helping the oppressed, being humble as opposed to proud and arrogant, forgiving those who offend us...the list is actually too long to list fully here, but you get the picture. Notice that most of these principles are relationally oriented. They teach us how to relate with others and with God.

We can change the spiritual atmosphere around us by loving, blessing, and being an encouragement everywhere we go. Many people love God, but when no one is looking, they can be guilty of mistreating or being mean to people. The fun part of focusing on blessing people is that, if you do these things regularly, the principle of sowing and reaping will eventually kick in. Your life will be overflowing with good things that you gave out to others, to the point that you cannot help but change the world around you. What you sow is what you will reap. If you sow grumbling, doubt, fear, depression, anxiety, and complaining, then that is what you will get in return. Developing a positive Kingdom perspective and lifestyle is what will truly change our lives and the lives of many around us.

My wife and I encountered a businessman who had an obvious problem with alcohol and lust. He was divorced and had health problems, but after listening to him talk, I was able to pick up on the fact that he enjoyed giving to good causes. In spite of the man's negative persona, we were able to encourage him that his desire to give to others was a good trait and a gift that God had given him. It was a small start to help him realize that he has a greater purpose and that God cares for him.

THE BREAKTHROUGH LIFESTYLE

We have looked at some very powerful yet simple principles that can radically change your life. But unless we put them into practice regularly they are just words on a page of a book on your shelf. Succeeding in life, even in relationship with God, is not automatic. Living life to the fullest requires developing a lifestyle that keeps you moving forward toward what God has for you.

The secret is simply to learn to make good choices on a daily basis. Make decisions to improve yourself and take steps every day— even very small ones—toward your goals or life dreams. God's destiny for your life will become clearer with every step! If you mess up, then confess it and get back on track right away.

Ever find yourself saying, "Someday I will…" Maybe you have heard the old saying, "The road called Someday leads to a town called Nowhere." For instance, you are reading this book as a result of a decision you made. Reading this book might help you change your life to some degree. But if you take the time to put into practice something that you are learning from it, then there is a better chance that you'll be radically transformed forever.

People buy books and training audios, but very few actually follow through with completing them. Studies show that if you just read or listen to someone telling you something, then you will only retain about 10 percent of what you heard after six weeks. If you do something practical to experience what you are learning, then you can accelerate your learning by retaining up to 80 percent or more. This is what will set you apart from millions of people everywhere.

Knowledge without application is not effective. People go to seminars and training classes to be taught more knowledge, but few people actually apply what they learn. Have you ever watched an infomercial on television for a new workout program like one of those new ab-miracle DVDs? Maybe you took a step to change by making a decision to buy it. But if you don't actually do what it teaches you, then it will not change your life beyond reducing your bank account and adding another DVD to your shelf.

After you try something new, you will need to take the next step of developing a new habit by doing that new thing consistently. For years, my own excuses were the biggest obstacle to doing things that I knew were good for me. I was too busy or too tired, and I did not need another thing to stress me out. But I noticed that when I put things off, they would begin to stack up. I would feel even more discouraged, and the simple task I needed to do now had extra weight on it and was harder to get to, so I put it off even more.

Getting backlogged on simple things like laundry, keeping your finances updated, exercising, even staying in touch with family or friends can lead to underlying feelings of guilt and discouragement. You might tell yourself that you need to wait until you have a full day to focus on the thing you've been putting off. Reality is that the full day rarely comes, and if it does, you're more likely to do something fun instead of dealing with the backlogged tasks.

I have developed a strategy that I call the *breakthrough lifestyle*. Maybe you have an idea of what you want in life, but you feel stuck. Or you have tried before, but gave up or had a bad experience. Here's some good news for you. The past only affects your present life if you allow it to. Each day is a fresh new start!

> **Past experiences do not dictate the present or the future—each day is a clean new start.**

Here's an example from my own life. Each week I do the exercise in Chapter 1; I pray and look for things that, if I would do them, would change my life for the better in some way. It does not have to be anything real big. Sometimes it is a relationship that needs attention, so I make a phone call or send an e-mail. Other times it may be a project that I am working on and I feel stuck, so I find someone who can give me advice or help with it. Maybe I am feeling sluggish, so I make sure that I am taking care of my body by exercising or changing my diet. By doing this regularly, in small bite-size steps, I have found a new freedom. I am still busy and tired and don't have much time to focus on new things. But a lifestyle of doing small things consistently brings good results over a period of time.

So what does taking steps to catch up on your backlogged tasks have to do with your destiny? If you can do small tasks consistently and not put them off, then you can handle the bigger opportunities and challenges when they come. You will be conditioned to respond and not avoid. Making positive changes is actually very easy once you get started. The biggest deterrent for most people is procrastination.

This book came about back in 2005, when I was thinking about the big task of researching and writing a book on helping people find their destiny. Since I travel a lot, I don't have a lot of time to write and research. I thought through some small steps that I could do regularly. It took a couple of years to accomplish, but I did it. Within two years I had completed the research, written the manuscript, and released the initial material in a course called *Accelerating into Your Life's Purpose,* which has helped thousands of people. Had I not made the decision to break through the discouragement of a big project by taking a few small steps, I would still be thinking about it and feeling guilty, and you would not be reading this book!

If changing your life is this simple, then why aren't more people doing it? It's not because of the level of difficulty or a lack of intelligence. Believe it or not, it is because most people are not aware that they can. They get so caught up in the day-to-day tasks of life, of making a living and staying busy, that they don't take the time to really sit down and consider what they want their life to look like. Most of what is happening in your life right now is the result of decisions you have made and the things that you do on a regular basis.

> *The secret to making positive changes in your life is learning to make good choices. This will involve finding ways to take steps to do the things that will better yourself—and to stop doing the things that are not good for you.*

The circumstances of your life are also influenced by what you believe you can do. God has no limits. Since you were created in God's image, then what you can accomplish through His Spirit, love, and power is unlimited. There really is nothing in your life that cannot be changed in some way. For instance, if you want to get in shape, it does not happen overnight. It is a process of doing things that take you toward it. The toughest part for most people is getting started.

When I was able to grasp this concept of a breakthrough lifestyle, my life began to change radically within a relatively short period of time. Think of it as doing one small thing a day, or even a week, toward something you want to achieve or accomplish. If you continue to do "one small thing" consistently—over two weeks, a month, six weeks, six months, and a year later—you will find yourself further along than you could have imagined. Eventually victories will begin to pile up instead of feelings of failure, and you will see extraordinary changes in your life. The best part is that people around you will take notice. You don't have to be a major planner or organizer. One of the weakest areas in my life is organization and following through. I have found ways to work around this and still get things done.

Sometimes you might feel hopeless to change because your situation is out of your control. For instance, you might be having difficulty at work because of your boss or another person. You can get another job, or you can at least change your attitude toward it. If you don't have the ability to change a situation because it is out of your control or involves others changing, then you can at least change your perspective and choose to view it differently.

> *Just as God is limitless—what you are capable of doing through God's power is unlimited.*

I hope you can catch my drift that life is not just about achievement and goals, but about transforming the quality of your life, finding your purpose, and ultimately doing what God has destined for your life. If you do it all in the context of God's love and power, you can't go wrong.

I got an e-mail from Sharnael Wolverton, a conference speaker and minister. She had been trying to write a book for over two years. She had the knowledge and abilities but was not sure why she could not get herself to write the book. Then she heard me speak on how to break through things that hold you back. I presented the exercise "What Are You Putting Off?" (see Chapter 1). She made a decision right then and there that she had to write the book, and, amazingly, she finished the manuscript in less than three weeks! Her problem was not in her ability; it was that she did not know how to start. Making that decision and taking one small step has resulted in two more books.

Learning to make decisions and take steps is what will change your life. Once you do it regularly, it will soon become automatic. This is a life-long journey, but it is simple just the same. It starts by making changes. Mother Teresa once said, "Small things done with great love can change the world." When you are able to transform the quality of your own life, you are then able to positively affect the lives of those around you.

Being proactive can get you to your destiny much faster. These are some things that will get you to your destiny: deepen your relationship with God; strengthen your ability to love; increase your character; and get a better understanding of your life calling.

> *It's not just about goals and results—it is also about changing the quality of your life—and finding your life purpose.*

Most people agree that developing this lifestyle of breaking through things that hold us back is good. To transform our lives we need to move beyond believing it is a good idea to actually doing it. This is what separates those who obtain their destiny from the ones who just talk about it.

EXERCISE: DO THE TURNAROUND

It is important to learn to turn negative situations around to be in line with God's perfect will for your life. It is similar to the Lord's Prayer, "On earth as it is in Heaven." We need to get a heavenly view of ourselves. As we do this, we will be in agreement with what God wants for us. God's ways are often opposite from ours. Based on the truth that "all things are possible" in God's Kingdom, we can turn around any situation for good.

1. Write down a few things that are currently negative in your life or seem impossible to change.

2. What is the opposite of the negative thing you are experiencing? If it is debt, then the opposite is wealth. If it is sickness, then the opposite is perfect health. Write the opposite down next to each of your negative things.

3. Pray and ask God to change your negative situation to positive. Begin to see yourself in this new light of God's perfect will for you. Continue to pray this new heavenly view of yourself until it comes into your mind more than the negative situation. Watch for God to change things and perform a miracle for you.

You can go to www.personaldevelopmentgodsway.com to download the exercise so that you can do it on your computer.

Chapter 4

BUILDING A GOOD FOUNDATION

BENEATH THE SURFACE

People everywhere want to discover their destiny or purpose in life.

A great place to start is to realize that *your destiny is shaped by what you do in your day-to-day life.* The things that you do on a regular basis build the foundation that your life is constructed on, whether positive or negative.

I tried to find a more recent movie that has an example of this principle, but the best I have seen is the movie, *Karate Kid.* Maybe you remember Mr. Miagi, who trained a young man named Daniel to do martial arts by first making him wax his car and paint a fence and other physical tasks. The movements he made by placing the "wax on" and taking the "wax off" were similar to the moves he needed to learn that later allowed him to win a karate championship.

In the Bible, David wanted to take on the giant named Goliath who was taunting the armies of Israel. David was younger and much smaller than others who had tried this task. He told the king that because he had killed lions and bears while shepherding his father's sheep, he was not afraid to go up against Goliath (see 1 Samuel 17:36). David did things privately during his regular job that put him in a position to take down the giant and move him into his destiny.

> **Your destiny is shaped in what you do in your day-to-day life.**

A few years ago my office was in Santa Monica, California, and a large building was being constructed across the street. On the street level, there was a fence with a picture of what the finished building would look like. But behind the scenes, there was a lot of mess and clutter as they dug the foundation. Unless you looked at the plans you would never know what the building was going to look like. Over a period of time and through a process of events, the building soon stood with a purpose to serve people. If the contractors had shortcut and built a faulty foundation, there would likely be trouble later on.

This analogy is very much like our lives. We do not always know what the end result will be. There may be times when we might be tempted to get things done quickly and cheaply, and not consider the consequences. It's important that we take the time to make sure our foundation is solid.

But everyone who hears these words of mine and does not put them into practice is like a foolish man who built his house on sand. The rain came down, the streams rose, and

*the winds blew and beat against that house, and it fell with
a great crash* (Matthew 7:26-27).

There are things that we can do in our personal life that can help prepare us for our future and help build a strong life foundation. I recommend starting each day with a positive focus. If you get up and begin right off the bat focusing on all the things you need to get done, chances are you will feel stressed. I like to think of this approach as eating a bowl of "Stress-O's" for breakfast. I used to live on stress and adrenalin. I was not always nice to be around either.

A better and more effective approach is to connect with God and yourself, and get a positive focus before you start. I was fortunate to learn this habit early on in my spiritual life. Whether in the morning, lunchtime, or evening, find what works for you based on your personality. I am a morning person so I get up early, but my wife stays up late, so she has her focus time after I go to bed or in the afternoon.

A lot of people these days tend to do things on the run. But spending specific time preparing and slowing down for just a few minutes can really help you in more ways than you may realize. Find what works best for you. If you don't have a quiet place at home, do what I did for a number of years. I found a place on the way to work where I could park my car and spend 10 to 15 minutes getting focused. Ask God to specifically guide you and give you what you need for that day.

*But seek first his kingdom and his righteousness, and all
these things will be given to you as well* (Matthew 6:33).

Set aside time to read the Bible. Prayer does not have to be formal or boring. I learned early in my spiritual life to incorporate this practice. I can't count the times in my life when the very thing I read that morning helped guide me in some way during the day. God wants to speak to us, and often this comes through the Bible. I am assuming that you may know how to incorporate this in your life to some degree. I know a lot of people agree that prayer and reading the Bible is good, but actually doing it is what counts!

One morning I was reading Psalm 37. I happened to be going to court that day to handle a legal issue. I was drawn to verse 33, *"...but the Lord will not leave them in their power or let them be condemned when brought to trial."* As I got to the court I found out the case was much more complicated than I had anticipated, and I really had wished I had consulted an attorney. Remembering the verse I read that morning, I had total peace as I went before the judge. The judge postponed the trial because my case number had been assigned to a closed case and they did not have the correct file, which gave me an extra three months to prepare.

There are many ways to connect with God. Sometimes I simply read through a section of the Bible. I often use a devotional guide or study book. If your focus time with God is boring or dry right now, then make a radical change. Try reading Psalms or Proverbs in a different translation of the Bible, like The Message or the New Living Translation. Get a study book or a devotional. Do something to disrupt your boredom and freshen things up.

POSITIVE STEPS TOWARD POSITIVE CHANGES

Quiet yourself to listen to God speaking to you. God usually speaks to us in a faint impression or small voice inside. People often hear God or get their ideas while in the shower because it is one of the few times they are truly quiet and away from distractions. Had I not slowed down to listen, I would have missed the times God spoke through an inner voice or guided me through an impression.

My wife and I knew that God was calling us to move to the central coast of California. I knew the general vicinity but did not know the city that we should move to. While praying one morning, out of the blue I heard God ask me in an internal voice, "What ship was Christopher Columbus on?" To be honest I had to Google it to find that it was the Santa Maria. We were soon offered an office at a church in Santa Maria.

Keep a journal or notebook. You can track the things that are happening in your life by writing them down. A life worth living is a life worth recording. You may want to track how God is speaking to you, answers to prayer, or the progress you make by reading this book. Most people are not aware of all that is happening in their lives because they don't track it. I actually have a personal thoughts journal, a dream journal, a writing journal, and an ideas and comedy journal. I have mine on my computer so that I can easily search it later and keep it password protected. Find what fits your personality. Maybe it is a book or looseleaf binder. Just do it.

Make a habit of recording your accomplishments. This may include things that you accomplish, answers to prayer, exciting things that happen. Quite often you are making headway and things are happening, but you fail to realize it. By taking time to celebrate your victories and accomplishments you are more likely to be encouraged and get excited. You can also use this as a way to learn from your mistakes by asking yourself how you could have done it or handled it differently.

Pay attention to the dreams you have at night. Even if you don't understand your dreams, quite often God speaks to you in your dreams. By writing your dreams down you can watch for patterns and you can refer back to them in the event that God speaks to you later about it. After years of study, I determined that our dreams at night often reveal our life dreams. I've devoted a chapter later in this book to hearing the voice of God and recognizing dreams that correlate with your destiny.

Take time to pray. Some people tell me that they are in a prayer conversation all day with God. Even still, it is good to take time and specifically focus yourself and talk with God. Take a prayer walk or drive in your car. Most people think they have to bow their head and close their eyes to pray. I don't recommend doing this while driving your car! God wants to be in close relationship with you. Your prayers do not always need to sound like a "to-do list" for God. I often converse with Him and pour out my heart and emotions. If you are more comfortable with writing, you can write prayers to God.

Listen to positive, uplifting music. Be sure to choose music that motivates and inspires you. Music can set the mood or change your emotional condition. I tend to listen to upbeat songs to start my day because it gives me more energy. I listen to slower, deeper worship music when I want to relax. With the popularity of the iPod, MP3 players, and Internet/satellite radio, we can take our favorite music with us wherever we go.

Listen to inspiring or educational training audios. Feed your mind and spirit in any way you can. I find that I don't always have time to read a lot of books, but audios are convenient when you are on the run, especially if you commute. Think of it as attending "Drive-Time University." Choose audios that will help you in all the areas of your life including your career, your emotional condition, your relationships, hobbies, etc. It is good to grow in all the areas of your life.

Capture creative ideas. Do something different or fun to get out of your routine. Often, a creative thought or idea floats through our minds, and we forget it later on. Consider carrying a small notepad or a digital voice recorder to record ideas or things you need to remember. Later you can transfer your notes into a journal or a to-do list. Another idea that I use often is to send a text message to myself from my cell phone, or I call my own voicemail and leave a message with something I want to remember. This works well for those people like me who tend to lose pieces of paper and notes.

Find ways to connect with God's creation. Nature is such an important aspect of a healthy life. Get out and breathe real air and not office or home air. Notice the beauty in things. Stop and enjoy animals and flowers and the clouds in the sky. This is a wonderful way to express your appreciation and love to God. I usually combine a walk with prayer because I can accomplish connection with God, creation, and exercise all at the same time. Sunshine and fresh air will do great things for you.

Connect with other people. We were created by God to live in a community of people. If you tend to spend time alone, go to lunch with a friend or co-worker. Connecting with others helps us to realize we are not alone in our struggles and our journey. If I ever have the option of going into a restaurant or using the drive-through, I go in. I do it for the extra exercise and to see people. You never know if you may run into someone who needs encouragement.

Live life now. It is easy to get focused too much on what things will look like in the future while we're searching out and trying to fulfill our destiny. We need to remember to enjoy each day. Time is a gift from God. It is something that we can never get back. We don't have to wait until we achieve a life goal or get the job of our dreams to feel as though we have actually lived.

There is a paradox of living a life of faith and expectancy, where we are praying and expecting a miracle for our situation to change, yet it looks like things are the same. Faith is required to get a vision for things that we don't see yet in our life. We don't want to give up on the future, but the challenge for us all is to find a balance between enjoying our life right now in the present while looking to the future to better ourselves.

The simple things done consistently will produce the greatest results in your life. The stronger the foundation you build in your life, the bigger the building you can construct. There are key principles that go into building a foundation, so take the time to build your foundation deep and solid.

THE THREE LOVES OF LIFE

One major component of a good life foundation is love. This is something we all know is good, but actually applying it in a practical way means that we need to take a look at our behavior and actions when no one else is looking. Test yourself to find out if you are exhibiting love in your life by noticing how you behave behind the wheel of your car. Do you treat people differently while you're driving than you would if you were walking? Imagine walking behind an elderly person on the sidewalk and yelling, "Hey, gramps, pick it up a little!" We tend to become more impersonal within the separated space of our cars.

Is being impatient with people really not loving them? Whenever I want to understand a subject deeper, I like to look in the Bible to see what Jesus had to say about it. The religious leaders of Jesus' day asked Him, *"What is the greatest commandment of all the Scriptures?"*

> Love the Lord your God with all your heart and with all your soul and with all your mind and with all your strength.' The second is this: 'Love your neighbor as yourself.' There is no commandment greater than these" (Mark 12:30-31).

If the greatest commandment of all time is love, then no matter what we do in life, if we build it on a foundation of love, we can't go wrong. I have read those verses many times before, but one day I took a deeper look and noticed that there are actually three separate types of love mentioned.

The first one is to love God. Most people love God, but deep down they might have some hidden anger about something. I used to spend a lot of time blaming God for all the bad things that happened to me and for all the war, disease, and death in the world. What kind of God would allow that? Then one day the answer came to me that God loves us so much that He gives us the freedom to choose or to reject His love. If God forced love on us, it would not be love at all.

Everyone on earth has the choice to receive God's love; sadly, there are people who will not receive it. They choose to be mean and harm others. There are evil, dark forces that do not want us to recognize the power of love. Bad things happen when people choose evil instead of love. You can decide to use bad situations when they happen to help develop your character.

I like to think of all the hard times I have experienced in my life as a gift that has helped train me. I would not like to experience them again, but how else would I know how to help others unless I made it through myself? Reality is that *"God is Love"* (1 John 4:8), and when you understand this part of His character, then you will not doubt God's motives.

The second type of love that Jesus mentioned is to love your neighbor. I think He was talking about loving more than the person next door, but learning to show love to others, including those in the car next to you. Loving other people means that you are kind, patient, and understanding. If everyone would show love, then we would have a world with less war and death from violence and even less disease.

Being kind and loving people takes effort and is often inconvenient. I mentioned earlier that one of the first places you will know whether you are truly loving others is noticing the way you act behind the wheel of your car. Seriously, I lived over 20 years in San Francisco and Los Angeles. I have probably spent a third of my life in traffic jams. When someone is driving erratically and cuts you off, the first thing you think of is probably not warm and loving thoughts. But what if the people in the car were on the way to the hospital because a family member was dying? Wow, that will change your view. I try to give people the benefit of the doubt.

Then again, there are still mean people out there. They are really just hurting, angry, and frustrated with their own life, so they take it out on the rest of us. I usually say a prayer for people like that and do my best not to get caught in their whirlwind of negativity. Be sure to not let someone else take your peace away.

The third type of love that Jesus mentioned is to love yourself. Most people may miss this one when reading this verse. It is so important for us to love ourselves. People who don't understand this suffer from low self-esteem. Then there are others who love themselves too much and lack humility or become prideful. Like everything there needs to be a balance to this.

But in John 13:34-35 (and again in 15:12-14), Jesus gave *His disciples* a new command,

> *"Love one another. **As I have loved you**, so you must love one another. By this all men will know that you are My disciples, if you have love for one another"* (John 13:34-35 TNIV).

I believe that this verse has been long overlooked and should be put into practice. To love others as He has loved us is the very resurrection power and revelation that truly transforms hearts! I'm just sayin'...

There is a Bible verse that, unfortunately, some Christians have taken a little too far. It is when John the Baptist said, Jesus must become greater and I must become less (see John 3:30). This was not meant to cause people to become insignificant to the point of not valuing themselves. Reality is that you cannot try to become less without being filled with more of the presence and goodness of God. If you try to become less without becoming more in Him, then the result will be that you will end up empty. This is actually false humility.

Loving yourself is important because you cannot give away love to others if you don't receive Jesus' love for yourself. If you want to know how much you love yourself, begin to notice your inner dialog. You may not realize it, but the things you say to yourself on a regular basis are what you actually believe, even if the statements are not true. Later in this book, I'll talk more about how to change your inner dialog and how to recognize thought patterns that can derail us from our destiny.

THE THREE GS OF LIFE

Let's look now at three spiritual principles that will help you build the foundation for your life. I call them the Three Gs.

The first is *Grace*. Grace is not just having poise or perfect balance. It is not just a prayer prayed before eating a meal. It is actually a quality of life that changes the world. Having grace is cutting people slack instead of cutting them down. It allows us to forgive others, which is a powerful principle in itself. Grace allows us to slow down enough to listen to others and to understand what they have been through and feel. Grace helps us develop patience and greater character that will set us apart.

God's love for us is given as a free gift with no requirements. This is often referred to as the grace of God. We need to extend this same grace to others.

*So in everything, do to others what you would have them
do to you...*(Matthew 7:12a).

The second G is *Gratitude*. When you have gratitude in your life,
you are thankful for everything. You realize that life is a gift every
day and not just another day to take for granted. You begin to look
for ways to love and connect with others because you are grateful for
all that you have received.

Gratitude is a sense of indebtedness to God and those around you.
You can never pay back God for your life, so you practice "paying
it forward" by freely giving to others. Gratitude allows you to see
the best in each situation and to be thankful for every part of your
life. Remember the movie *Pay it Forward*? A twelve-year-old named
Trevor believed in the goodness of people, and was determined to
change the world for the better by doing nice things. People who
received the kind acts were so grateful that they began to help others,
and it resulted in a huge change.

The apostle Paul mentions that he learned a secret to be content...
that is gratitude.

*I know what it is to be in need, and I know what it is
to have plenty. I have learned the secret of being content
in any and every situation, whether well fed or hungry,
whether living in plenty or in want* (Philippians 4:12).

Gratitude goes hand-in-hand with the third G, *Generosity*.
Generosity goes way beyond the spiritual principle of giving. You may
have heard it said, *"The more you give, the more you receive"* (Acts
20:35). As this principle begins to take root in your life, you will
move from giving in order to get, to giving because it is good. It feels
so good to give. You come to a place where you give because it helps

others, because it is the flow of life. Giving creates an attraction in your life that draws blessing back to you.

Unfortunately, there are some preachers and television evangelists who have used manipulation to get people to give to their church or ministry, bless their hearts. This causes people to have a bad experience with the idea of giving freely for the right reasons. The principle of generosity and giving goes way beyond money. It is giving of your time, energy, love, attention, and your resources. It is helping someone in need, not because you owe them one, but simply because they are in need.

> *Give, and it will be given to you. A good measure, pressed down, shaken together and running over, will be poured into your lap. For with the measure you use, it will be measured to you* (Luke 6:38).

PRINCIPLE OF SOWING AND REAPING

Grace, gratitude, and generosity are important parts of a spiritual principle: Whatever you sow you will reap (see Galatians 6:7). What you do comes back to you eventually. This does not apply to sin that we repent of. Most people are not conscious of how much this principle influences them, because there is a delay factor involved. You will not harvest the things you plant until sometime later. So what you do on a day-to-day basis will not normally affect your life until later on. If you begin doing good things on a daily basis—like love, grace, gratitude, and generosity—later your life will be overflowing with these same qualities. It will start coming back to you continually, as long as you keep giving.

This is one of the quickest ways to see change in your life. Begin now to intentionally give away love, grace, and gratitude and be as generous as you can. If you do it consistently, you will begin to see people treat you differently, and things will start flowing your way.

A colleague of mine, Tom, used to complain about the airlines he had to fly for business. He was always getting a bad middle seat in the back of the plane next to a crying baby. Then I reminded him of the principles I am sharing with you. He started putting in compliments to the flight attendants and being grateful for the fact that he can fly and not have to drive. Not only did his attitude change, but he got over 25 free first-class upgrades in one year, not from complaining but from changing the spiritual atmosphere around him. Tom began to give positive things like love, grace, gratitude, and generosity. His life foundation was strengthened, and he had a good time as well.

There are so many things that you can accomplish in life. Things like starting a business, going to school, getting married and having a family, buying a house, writing a book, getting out of debt, losing weight, or whatever it is for you! Be sure to build it on a foundation of: love, grace, gratitude, and generosity. Build your foundation on a close relationship with God, and your plans will succeed and your life will be filled with meaning.

EXERCISE: STRENGTHEN YOUR FOUNDATION

What can you do today to help strengthen your life foundation? Remember that your destiny is formed by the things you do day to day. It will take practice to get in the habit of doing some of the things we discussed in this chapter. After you do them regularly, they will become automatic and you won't have to think about them.

Start your day by asking the following:

1. Who can I show love to today?

2. Who can I have grace for today? Think about someone who gets on your nerves or bugs you. Find a simple way to bless them.

3. What am I grateful for today?

4. How can I show generosity today?

5. Take a moment and examine the things that you do on a regular basis that connect you with God. Are there any changes you can make that will enrich your experience?

6. Share what you are learning so far with at least three people. Be sure to tell someone each time you make a commitment to doing something new. Having accountability and another perspective will help you change much more quickly.

You can go to www.personaldevelopmentgodsway.com to download the exercise so that you can do it on your computer.

Chapter 5

PURPOSE AND DESTINY

I meet a lot of people as I speak at conferences and training events. I have the opportunity to observe people from all walks of life and hear their stories. People ask me most often about how they can know their destiny. "How can I know for sure what it is that I am supposed to do in life?" Many people are saying that they feel stuck and don't know what to do next.

People often come to my events or hire me as their coach, and they want me to tell them what to do or what their destiny is. Even if I knew what it was and told them, their life probably would not change much. This is because most of us learn from experience, and we grow from the journey. When you discover it yourself, you are more likely to feel an ownership and do what it takes to get there. You are the only one who will be able to fulfill your destiny. What I've found is that most people already have what they need to either get started or take the next step in their destiny. They just need encouragement to move forward.

Life purpose and destiny are like a "connect the dots" drawing. The picture may not be all that clear at first, but your job is to find the next dot. You can't skip through to the end. I want to encourage you that if you feel frustrated or dissatisfied with your life or your current situation, you may very well be on the right track. Dissatisfaction is not always bad because it can drive you to find more. Most people either find something in life to inspire them with passion to achieve it, or they get so desperately dissatisfied that they set out on a journey to find their purpose. It does not matter whether you are motivated by inspiration or desperation. What counts is to take steps to do something about it.

> **Dissatisfaction is not bad because it can drive us to find more in life.**

Here are some examples from the Bible in which people used dissatisfaction to drive them to discover their greater purpose in God. Jacob was dissatisfied that Laban was profiting off of him, which caused him to take action that enabled him to go back and face his brother. Daniel was dissatisfied with being in captivity, so he searched the writings of the prophet Jeremiah and found that the captivity was about to end. So he took it upon himself to pray repentance for Israel and ask God to release them from captivity. Nehemiah was dissatisfied that the walls of Jerusalem had not been rebuilt, so he approached the king to receive permission to lead the rebuilding project. The walls were rebuilt in 52 days.

There is a particular story from the Bible that comes to mind that really demonstrates how people can feel dissatisfied and use their frustration to radically turn things around. It is David and his mighty men. David's destiny was to be king of Israel, but there was an evil king ruling who opposed him and even tried to take his life. David needed help getting into his calling. All he had was a group of men who were outcasts of the religious society, yet they were able to do incredible things once they hooked up with David. The description of the motley crew did not sound all that mighty.

> *All those who were in distress or in debt or discontented gathered around him [David], and he became their leader. About four hundred men were with him* (1 Samuel 22:2).

Even though there were only 400, they could fight armies that outnumbered them because they were focused with a vision and God was with them. It is interesting to note the description of this group was similar to many people today: distressed, in debt, and discontented.

God wants us to get in touch with the possibilities of what could happen if we get a clear vision, a passion, and a purpose to live. God wants to empower us with purpose.

The result is that we not only find something to live for, we find something worth dying for as well. Finding destiny and purpose in life is important because it fills the longing we all have inside to express more of who we are and why we were created. It creates a desire to be part of something bigger than our selves. Maybe you feel that you have something to give or express that could help others. We all want to know that our life has purpose, especially if we have suffered. Wouldn't it be great to know that our painful experiences were not in vain, but can be used to help someone else who is going through something similar?

WHAT IS YOUR LIFE PURPOSE?

I have heard many different definitions for life purpose. To sum it up, your life purpose involves a unique assignment from God that includes developing yourself spiritually and growing in godly character. In the process, you can help others do the same. If we all would commit ourselves to this process, we would have a much higher quality of life and would ultimately make the world a better place to live.

No matter what you do in life, what career you pursue, or what you are working toward, your purpose is to grow and mature in all areas of your life: spiritually, emotionally, and relationally. Your personal growth must be made a priority, not just something you do like going to church once or twice a week. This concept echoes the message of Jesus in three classic statements He made that are in the Bible:

> *No matter what we do in life, what career we pursue, or what we are working toward, our purpose is to grow, increase in character, and help others do the same.*

- Jesus said, *"Come and follow me..."* (Matthew 4:19). You can't follow Jesus long without bringing some type of change to your life. When we begin to follow Jesus, we are making our personal growth a priority.

- Jesus also said, *"Love God with all your heart and strength, and love your neighbor as yourself"* (Matthew 22:37-40). When we love God, ourselves, and others we can't avoid developing strong godly character.

- And some of His final words were to *"...teach people to obey what I have taught you"* (Matthew 28:19-20).

If you have learned anything in the process of following Jesus, you can help others.

WHAT DID JESUS SAY ABOUT PURPOSE?

One of the first statements Jesus spoke publicly at the start of His ministry is much more profound than most people realize.

"Come, follow me," Jesus said, "and I will make you fishers of men" (Mark 1:17).

He said this to some common, everyday fishermen that later became His disciples and eventually leaders. Jesus was a religious teacher, but notice that He did not say they had to become professional teachers or rabbis to follow Him. God wanted to use them in the way they were created. They were fishermen, and Jesus said that they could become fishers of men. God wants to use you uniquely in the special way that you were already created. Your purpose and the journey to obtain it will be unique based on your distinctive characteristics and life experiences.

YOU ARE UNIQUELY CREATED

God created each of us to be individuals. There is no DNA that is identical, no fingerprint or snowflake, no two things in creation that are exactly alike. Think about the process you have already gone through to be created. The journey of your father's specific sperm to get to your mother's egg is about a 1 in 500 million chance. So you have already won the race! Had another sperm cell made it before yours then you would not be you, but another entirely different person. You are not only unique, but you were born a winner!

What makes us all unique is not only the way we were created but the way we were raised and the experiences we have had. It is not always the people with the right upbringing, education, or status who actually make it in life. I used to think that I could not be successful because I did not go to college. I grew up in an area of the country that placed a high value in hiring people with college degrees as opposed to the right person for the job. That was a big obstacle for me to get past, but when I stopped letting it hold me back and started focusing on the uniqueness of how God created me, I became successful at nearly everything that I did.

Since we were all uniquely created for a purpose, let's look deeper into why we were created. This allows us to understand God's intentions for us and gives us some ideas and guidelines on how to pursue a deeper relationship with Him. We were created in God's image, and since He created the world, we too have an inherent desire to create as well. We need to see that our purpose and destiny is achieved by co-laboring with God.

FIVE REASONS YOU WERE CREATED

1. You were created uniquely by God, if for no other reason than to be loved by Him—you don't have to repay God for the life that has been given to you. It simply brings God pleasure to give you life. It is important to realize that God is not angry with you, nor does He hate you. First John 4:16 says that God is love.

2. You were created to function as part of a community. You need other people—friends, family, co-workers—to stay spiritually, emotionally, and relationally healthy. And they need you as well (see Romans 12:4-5).

3. A major part of why you were created is to grow and mature. Unfortunately, many people go to school to learn, and when they get out they stop learning. We were created by God to continually improve and grow. Committing yourself to continual improvement will help you advance to your destiny much faster (see Philippians 3:12-14).

4. You were created to contribute to something greater than yourself. Contribution is a major component of our human needs. When you reach out beyond yourself, you connect with the very nature of God in you (see Luke 10:30-37).

5. You were ultimately created to find and fulfill your purpose and destiny in life (see Ephesians 2:10).

WHAT'S THE DIFFERENCE BETWEEN PURPOSE AND DESTINY?

It's sometimes difficult to distinguish between purpose and destiny. You'll notice that I use these terms interchangeably. This is not to confuse you. The fact is that destiny and purpose are very closely related. *Purpose* is the assignment from God to grow and improve ourselves and help others do the same. Purpose is more what you do in life and who you become. *Destiny* is the direction you go with it. Your destiny is your "destination" or where you end up, whether it is positive or negative.

This is easy to see in the life of Elvis Presley. He loved to sing gospel music, and his life purpose was to encourage people with his gift of music. The direction that Elvis took with his talent truly blessed and encouraged a lot of people. It was not, however, the level of spiritual impact that God had intended for him in my opinion. So his destiny brought him eventually to an unfulfilled state in which he took drugs and overate to numb the pain. He obtained his life purpose, but the direction he took brought him to a destiny of destruction. Had Elvis discovered his higher purpose in God, his life would have been more satisfying to him, he would not have gotten on drugs, and he may still be alive today.

Finding your destiny and purpose is a journey or process that, if you make it a priority, you will find a way to get there. Doing nothing at all brings you to a destiny of dissatisfaction and feelings of failure. Destiny and purpose are the things that you were created by God to do or accomplish. God has a high calling and purpose for everybody.

Your destiny is based on how you respond to what God already desires for you.

FREQUENTLY ASKED QUESTIONS ABOUT DESTINY

Here are a few questions I get asked about destiny.

The most common is, "Do we all have a specific destiny to fulfill in life?" Yes we do, but it may change depending on our ability to grow in maturity. Remember that our life purpose is to grow personally and spiritually and help others do the same. God's desire might be for you to help thousands of people get set free from the pain of abuse. Then through a series of events and tests along the way, if you did not achieve the maturity level required for such a great task, God may choose to readjust your destiny based on what you can handle at the level you are now. You will still be helping people, but not necessarily to the degree that God originally intended for you. You might be helping dozens or hundreds of people, as opposed to thousands.

People also tell me that they feel like there is something more to their life, but they don't know what it is. This is because destiny usually builds over time. I am convinced that God has been giving us clues all of our life about what we are called to do. Often it is what we are already naturally good at or have passion for. It is not to say that you can run out and achieve anything you desire and assume it is God's will for your life. But most of the time your uniqueness is pointing you toward your life purpose.

Destiny reveals itself through things you are excited about and sometimes through dissatisfactions, failures, longings, intuition, vision, and drive for something more. Dissatisfaction and a longing for something more will often drive you to find a way to something new. It might be through training, education, job change, or counseling that you find your true path.

Whenever I talk about destiny, I get questions about marriage. I often hear people say they feel destined to marry a particular person. Is it true that we can have a soul mate? The notion of a "soul mate" was made popular over 2,000 years ago by the Greek philosopher Plato. He surmised that a perfect human being was tragically split in two, resulting in a race of creatures sentenced to spend the rest of their lives searching for that missing other who can complete them.

I don't agree with the philosophy that we need another person to make ourselves whole. It is God who makes us an integrated person, and we are a whole person already. God can bring us to the ideal mate. I do need to mention that even if it were God's will and intention for you to marry a person and he or she says no, then it is now null and void. God may have intended for you to be with someone, but He will not force His will on the other person. The person has the right to choose. If he or she does not respond positively, then you can trust that God will bring someone else who will still be His will for you.

Some people tell me that they will not date anyone because they are waiting for God to bring the right mate to them. Some of these people have been waiting for years and have not met anyone. Be sure God has spoken this to you clearly and you are not pulling back because of fear. Dating can actually be healthy and allow you to learn more about your likes and dislikes. People often ask me if we can miss our destiny. Yes, we sure can. But God is always faithful to give us something else as we return to pursuing Him for the direction in our life. Destiny always requires some type of sacrifice and concerted effort. It might be years of study and practice, or giving up other dreams to pursue it.

Here is a good example of someone missing their destiny in the Bible. In Luke 18:18-25, Jesus was nearing the end of His ministry on earth with only a few weeks left before He was to fulfill His destiny by dying on the cross. A rich young leader asked Him what he should do to inherit eternal life. Jesus answered him with the steps he needed to take and then went on to tell him that he lacked one thing: He needed to give his money to the poor and follow Him.

It is interesting that Jesus uses the same words, *"Follow me"* that He did when He called Peter, James, and John to be disciples (see Matthew 4:19). The young man went away discouraged because it would have cost him all his wealth. Some people think that Jesus was telling us that we cannot have wealth. I like to take a different angle. I think that this rich young man would most likely have been the replacement for Judas, who handled the finances for Jesus' ministry. Judas was the one who betrayed Jesus and later hanged himself. Jesus may very well have been trying to "headhunt" a successor for Judas as one of the 12 disciples.

Since the young leader had not been following Jesus for three years like the rest, Jesus may have been trying to fast-track him into being a disciple. This would have required the man to get through the things that have held him back. In his case, it was the love of money. The rich young man missed his destiny in God. He was afraid of losing his earthly possessions. As he walked away, Jesus made a promise:

> *"I tell you the truth," Jesus said to them, "no one who has left home or wife or brothers or parents or children for the sake of the kingdom of God will fail to receive many times as much in this age and, in the age to come, eternal life"* (Luke 18:29-30).

With God there is always another chance! Many people never reach true fulfillment in life because they give up on goals and dreams. Often a destiny that we sense God calling us to may seem too big for us to believe or achieve. High destiny callings always require time and effort to develop. Most people give up during the training and testing process.

> **High destiny callings always require time and effort to develop. Most people give up during the training and testing process.**

The things I am now accomplishing in my life were all beyond what I thought was possible when I started. In fact, they seemed impossible. I made a lot of mistakes along the way, and I still make mistakes. But I am well on my way to fulfilling my destiny, and it came by making decisions to get serious! I had tried to get into my destiny so many times before and failed and gave up. In 1991, I decided that I would not go back or give up again. I was going for all that God had for me. My life has radically changed since then.

GOD'S GOOD INTENTIONS FOR YOU

Quite often we are not able to see our purpose and destiny, so we are required to rely on faith. The principle of faith allows us to trust that there is something special and unique for us, even if our experiences have been opposite. Sometimes there is great resistance or even setbacks before we are able to get into the fullness of God's desires for us.

> *Now faith is being sure of what we hope for and certain of what we do not see* (Hebrews 11:1).

We need to live this principle and be certain of God's intentions for us, even though we may not see them yet. Here's another powerful biblical principle:

> *"For I know the plans I have for you," declares the Lord, "plans to prosper you and not to harm you, plans to give you hope and a future"* (Jeremiah 29:11).

These are God's intentions for us. His plans are to prosper us, give us a hope and a future. If you read on, you'll see the benefits of grasping this.

> *Then* [after you find God's plans] *you will call upon me and come and pray to me, and I will listen to you. You will seek me and find me when you seek me with all your heart* (Jeremiah 29:12-13).

When you seek God's plans and purpose and do not give up, you will come to a place where things become clearer and you will find a deeper relationship with God in the process. Your prayers will be answered more readily because you are getting into synchronization with God's purpose for your life. It is as though you know what to pray and when. It is very clear that answered prayer and a closer relationship with God are all linked to finding your purpose and pursuing your destiny.

SEEING OURSELVES AS GOD SEES US

If you are to stop allowing negative things from your past control your present and future, it will involve changing old thought patterns.

> *Do not conform any longer to the pattern of this world, but be transformed by the renewing of your mind. Then you will be able to test and approve what God's will is—his good, pleasing and perfect will* (Romans 12:2).

Renewing your mind involves replacing the old mind-set with a new one. Your new mind-set is who you are becoming, not who you were. The good news is that this is the way that God sees you. When you come into line with God's intentions, you actually tap into His unlimited power to transform your life.

Here's how it works. I mentioned previously that God's intention for you is to prosper you, give you hope and a future, and not harm you (see Jeremiah 29:11). If you try to make changes in your life by focusing on what you should not do, then you are trying to live by rules and not by a relationship with God. God is relationship oriented. His own description of Himself is that of a Father, which indicates that He wants to relate to us as family.

The Bible compares this transformation to stepping away from the picture of your old self and putting on a picture of your new self. God's focus is on you becoming who you were created to be. He relates to you according to this image. It is very important that you see yourself in this way as well.

One of the apostle Paul's prayers for those he was training was that the eyes of their heart would be enlightened and that they would know the hope of their calling (see Eph. 1:18). The Greek word used for "know" is to "see or perceive." This goes deeper than just head-knowledge. When you see and perceive the hope of your calling, it causes you to take action because it is much more tangible and real.

God sees us as we are becoming or in our full potential. Here are some examples from the Bible of this concept.

Judges 6: Gideon is hiding in fear, and an angel comes and calls him a mighty man of valor—God treated him the way He saw him in the future.

John 1:40-42: Simon had just met Jesus, and he was still flaky—Jesus says you shall be called Cephas (or Peter, which means "rock"). Jesus treated him the way He saw him in the future, not how he was at that moment.

Acts 9: Saul was murdering Christians, and then God knocked him to the ground on the road to Damascus. Before Saul's life was changed, God told Ananias to tell Saul that he is a chosen instrument and is a brother.

A real life example is someone like Nancy, who never saw herself as a leader, let alone a business owner. She was a stay-at-home mom, then her son went off to college, and she was challenged with finding the greater purpose for her life. She began getting clues about her destiny by asking others. One day she was able to get a glimpse that her potential in God had no limits. She began pursuing a dream of owning a corner store in her hometown. She got a business plan, and an SBA loan that took over two years. In the process she worked as a manager of a coffee shop to gain experience. She was able to start seeing herself as a leader, even though she had not led anything since high school.

The key is to begin to see yourself in your full potential in God. See yourself as God sees you, not as you once were or even as you are now, but by faith getting a picture of who you are becoming in God. You might not be there yet, but if you begin seeing yourself there, then you will start changing your behavior to act differently. You will start coming into agreement with God for your life calling.

EXERCISE: DISCOVER CLUES ABOUT YOUR DESTINY

God created you unique and with a special purpose. His intentions for you are nothing but the best. Sometimes there are hidden clues about our destiny in the things we value and are naturally good at. This does not mean that everything you like to do is necessarily God's ultimate will.

You may want to go to a private place and put on some uplifting or inspiring music as you do this. We are going to take a look at where you are and what excites you. Don't be formal—just let your pen or keyboard flow and write down as many things as you can think of, and find one that strikes you inside.

1. Make a list of a few characteristics about yourself that are unique. State them in the positive. Brainstorm a list of at least five to ten for each. Example: I am creative, I am funny, I am a positive influence.

2. What are your current strengths? Example: helpful to others, encourage others, a visionary, an organizer, etc.

3. What are some of your weaknesses? Example: difficult time saying no, get too busy, unorganized, etc.

4. Make a full list of your accomplishments and things you are proud of. This is not a formal list; come up with as many things as you can think of. If you can't think of any, then go back to learning to ride a bike or getting a bowling trophy in the 8th grade, then move

to your career, relationships, family, marriage, spiritual, etc. Try to come up with 25 or more. Circle 5 of these events that made a major impact on your life.

5. Make a list of things that excite you. What are you passionate about? You are not writing a formal mission statement here—this is an exercise to clear your head of all the formal ideas about destiny and the things that we have been programmed about how it should look. Examples: wind surfing, roller coasters, having friends over, painting, writing, business, etc. Be specific. Don't just say I am passionate about my family. Describe what it is specifically, such as I am passionate about seeing my children fulfill their destiny.

6. What can you learn about yourself based on this exercise? Write a paragraph or two about the insight you gain about what excites you, what you have accomplished, your uniqueness, and anything else you have picked up about yourself during this exercise. Write it in the third person—as if you were reporting about someone else. It is time to toot your horn for just a minute. Have fun with this, even though it might feel awkward. Resist writing who you want to be or who you are in Christ. This is who you are as a person created by God.

You can go to www.personaldevelopmentgodsway.com to download the exercise so that you can do it on your computer.

Chapter 6

REMOVING OBSTACLES

As we cruise down life's highway toward our destiny, we may encounter some bumps in the road. There will be obstacles to prepare for in order to overcome them. Some are self-imposed and others are so common to our society that we may not recognize them as potential problems at first. Later, we'll get into how to fast track into your future by minimizing things that short circuit us and replacing them with short cuts that help us get through the speed bumps.

WE NEED TO RISE ABOVE MEDIOCRITY

Let's jump right in and look at a very serious destructive pattern that holds millions of people back from growing and advancing to maturity. It is learning to take full responsibility for your actions and your life. Sounds simple, but believe me, many people miss this one. Too many people settle for an average life of mediocrity.

But there are things that you can do to pursue a balanced and healthy life that is full of meaning. When you apply the principles I am sharing with you, your life will stand out from others.

The apostle Paul compares our spiritual life with running a race with the intention to win:

> *Do you not know that in a race all the runners run, but only one gets the prize? Run in such a way as to get the prize* (1 Corinthians 9:24).

In other words, don't settle for less from yourself. Give life your all. Unfortunately, our society conditions us not to succeed. Have you ever noticed what happens when someone at work or school excels? Others start to talk about them, calling them the teacher's pet or the kiss-up, because when people see someone else succeeding, they feel guilty about their own life. So they subconsciously try to drag the successful person back down to their standards.

I told the story earlier about when I worked as a middle manager for a company that decided to invest in educating the staff by sending us to a series of leadership development courses. They offered this opportunity to others, but not many wanted to go because it was over the weekend and involved a lot of preparation and tests. I loved it and came back to work and applied everything I learned. Suddenly, I was known as the "get it done guy" in the company. People came to me all the time to help them resolve problems at work. At one point I became the department turnaround specialist because I had an ability to see the big picture. Then at the end of the year the company gave out production awards. I got nearly all of them, including employee of the year and a big bonus. Suddenly, my coworkers began to treat me differently. Some of them stopped associating with me, and it would get quiet when I walked into the lunch room.

Two years later, the company went bankrupt when the owner's family embezzled the company's funds. The bank seized all the assets and brought in a turnaround team of consultants to run the company and try to save it from closing completely. Most of management was fired, but I was selected to be part of the new management team, mainly because I was willing to pursue excellence.

Because of the experience I gained during that time, I was able to move into an entirely new career in consulting. I went from $25 per hour to $125 per hour nearly overnight, and I don't have a college education. It pays to apply yourself and keep a good attitude. I was not out for promotion or to make money. I told them that I would do whatever they wanted me to do. My motivation was to do what God wanted me to do to the best of my ability.

If you really want to change your life, then work at your job as if you are working for God. This is a powerful spiritual principle:

> *Whatever you do, work at it with all your heart, as working for the Lord, not for men, since you know that you will receive an inheritance from the Lord as a reward. It is the Lord Christ you are serving* (Colossians 3:23-24).

I would bet that the majority of the people in your life are settling for mediocrity. When people are bored with their lives, they too often sit around complaining instead of doing something constructive. Talk radio is a good example of this bad habit. Negative results follow when criticism is shared and few solutions are offered. Talk radio is usually designed for angry people to vent. I prefer not to listen to the shows that get really negative. When I do, I find myself feeling angry and helpless at the same time, because it feels like there is injustice happening and there is nothing we can do about it.

NO LONGER A VICTIM

Most of us were raised in a blame-shift environment. We may not recognize it because it is so common. People are always blaming something or someone else instead of finding another way to get the job done. We learn as children to make up an excuse instead of owning up to it. As adults we will continue to make excuses unless we intentionally choose to change this pattern.

The first step to changing ourselves is to recognize that there is a problem with grumbling and making excuses. Excuses are disempowering, especially when we start believing them. We become victims and lose our creativity for problem solving. You can recognize that you are doing this when you deflect any advice people give you. It is good to kindly thank someone for attempting to help you, and be sure to pray about what they are saying in case it may be revealing a blind spot you may have.

My wife is a marriage and family therapist. She is not my therapist, but she sure helps me a lot. When we first got married, I said one day, "You make me angry." She replied, "I don't have that kind of power over you to make you feel a certain way. You are choosing to feel angry." Wow, that was a breakthrough for me. I realized that no one could make me feel or do something because in reality I have a choice. Once I realized that I had choices, I was able to relate to others differently.

Here are a few examples of blame shifting. People might say that they are not able to save any money because they have too many bills to pay, which places the blame on the bills, as opposed to their financial responsibility. The reality is that they could spend less or make more. When someone tells me that they can't get ahead financially because they pay too much in rent and taxes, I suggest that they move to a cheaper place and consult with a tax expert to make sure they aren't paying too much in taxes. How about when people say they don't have enough time to exercise? I wonder how much television they watch. You can always do a few exercises in front of the tube. One thing we all have in common is time. You get the idea.

When we take responsibility for our actions and situations, we gain back control. We always have choices. If you are not able to change a situation, then you can at least change the way you respond to it. You have a choice!

WE ALL HAVE A STORY

Ever notice how some people thrive on drama and attention? It boils down to wanting to feel loved. We are a very "therapeutic society." We now have a diagnosis for nearly everything. Some people have a note from their doctor to justify their unhealthy behavior because of something that happened to them in the past. Everyone has a story, and some are more tragic than others. I'm not dismissing the very real effect that emotional wounding or abuse can have on us. I'm just saying that we can choose to seek healing to become whole and strong, or we can choose to view our circumstances as excuses to complain and view ourselves as victims and stay stuck there all our lives.

I once found myself making excuses for my behavior. Some people say things like, I am a pastor's kid; I was physically abused; I was molested; my parents were alcoholics; I grew up in a bad side of town; my family did not have the money to send me to college; or my dog ran away. Our story can become like a breaker switch, automatically shutting us down and hindering us when we get under pressure. This can happen when we begin to grow and succeed as well.

A breaker switch controls the amount of electricity or power that can flow through a current. If too much comes through, it automatically shuts itself off. I actually have a very tragic life story. I suffered from emotional, physical, and sexual abuse growing up. I love and honor my parents, and they did so many great things for me, but I grew up in a home with alcoholics, and we moved over 17 times while

I was still in elementary school. I could go on and on about the negative stuff in my past. I have a Ph.D. in excuses!

I spent over a decade of my life in a therapist's office working through my issues. For the longest time, I unintentionally used my story from the past to justify my own bad behavior and why I could not succeed. Whenever someone would accidentally trip over one of my wounds, I felt justified to act in any way I wanted because it was not my fault: I was abused. This attitude can really hinder your relationships with people and your ability to succeed.

> *You cannot change the past, but you can change the way it affects you in the present.*

To some degree we all have something from the past that tries to stop us from our destiny. There is a time for healing and grieving, but don't stay in the emotional recovery room too long. You cannot change the past, but you can change the way it affects you in the present. When you change your behavior in the present, you are then changing your future.

TAKING RESPONSIBILITY FOR EVERYTHING YOU DO

When we use excuses, we are being a victim. Victims think they have no control over what happens to them. They allow themselves to be controlled by the things that happen around them. A victim mentality blinds you to your own faults, causes you to think everyone is out to get you, blames your problems on others because of their decisions or actions, keeps you in a continual spinning cycle that has no end, and can cause you to be addicted to the attention you get when you share your latest drama.

When you are a victim, you allow the past to keep controlling you. When you take responsibility, you gain control back in your life.

We will never be able to stop "stuff" that happens to us, *but we can change the way we respond to it.* Let's face it; life is full of pain and problems. They will never go away totally, but we can adjust how we respond to them and decrease their negative influence in our lives. The first step to taking 100 percent responsibility for your life is to give up *all* your excuses. The past is the past—the pain does not need to last.

LEARNING TO ASK THE RIGHT QUESTIONS

When God created the human brain, He created a massive super-computer. We were all born with our brains ready to be programmed with memories, rules, and experiences. Yes, we have a soul and a spirit as well, but for teaching purposes, think of your mind as a computer screen. When you ask yourself a question, it is like typing it into a computer and pressing the search button. Then your brain will search its memory banks and give you an answer to most any question you ask it.

For instance, you might ask yourself, "Why am I so stupid?" Your brain will search your memory and give you examples of negative and embarrassing memories and experiences to validate what you think about yourself. When something happens to hurt you, the typical question you might ask is, "Why do bad things always happen to me?" Your brain will gladly give you a reinforcing answer to help keep you trapped in a negative cycle.

A better way to ask yourself questions would be, "How did I allow that to happen?" or "What can I do in the future to prevent that?" By changing our perspective on our problems, we get ourselves to find new solutions instead of validating old behaviors that no longer serve us. It takes practice, but you can turn this part of your thinking around and transform your mind to be aligned with God's will for your life. Begin daily to practice asking your brain solution-seeking questions.

DESTINY COMES THROUGH SUCCESS AND FAILURE

Success and failure are all in how you view them. I used to think that I failed if I did not accomplish something I set out to do. Maybe you did something like eating a Big Mac hamburger 3 days into a 21-day fast. Did you really fail? Or were you tempted and hungry? Get back up, brush off the sesame seeds, and make it an 18-day fast!

> *Destiny comes through success and failure.*

Thomas Edison tried for years, through thousands of failed experiments, before he got an incandescent light bulb to work properly. He never considered any experiment that did NOT work as a failure. Instead, every experiment that did not work was one more way toward how not to invent an incandescent bulb.

Colonel Sanders, who founded Kentucky Fried Chicken, was rejected by over 1,000 restaurants and diners before someone agreed to carry his "finger lickin' good" secret fried chicken recipe. The key was that he did not give up.

My life has had more failure than success, but I have made a commitment that quitting is not an option. I now view failure as a necessary training event that will prepare me for something in the future. I actually have changed the way I think so that I am no longer impacted by failure. I now believe that I am successful if I have learned anything in the process that will help me to reach my overall destiny. So you can make mistakes and still be successful in the bigger picture of things.

Joey Green, in the book *The Road to Success Was Paved With Failures,* found some interesting cases of people who did not succeed at first:

> If at first you don't succeed…welcome to the club. Feel that life is passing you by? That others are getting ahead while you aren't? Don't despair. Riches and renown may still lie in your future.
>
> After all, consider the experiences of…
>
> - Walt Disney, whose first cartoon production company went bankrupt
>
> - Barbra Streisand, who made her New York stage debut in a show that opened and closed in a single night
>
> - Edgar Allan Poe, who was expelled from West Point
>
> - Elvis Presley, whose high school music teacher gave him a C and told him he couldn't sing
>
> - Jane Fonda, who was kicked out of the Girl Scouts for telling dirty jokes
>
> - John F. Kennedy, who ran for president of his college class and lost

- John Grisham, whose first novel, *A Time to Kill*, was rejected by 16 agents and a dozen publishing houses[1]

> *There are life-lessons for us all to learn and if we learn them quicker—we can significantly cut the time to get to our destiny.*

Many people who have found their destiny seem to find it later in life. This does not need to be the case. There are life lessons for us all to learn, and, if we learn them more quickly, then we can significantly cut the time to get to our destiny. I will go into this more later, but there are things you can do today to prepare you for tomorrow.

THE SPIN CYCLE

I have noticed that as we start moving toward our purpose and destiny, or anything that will better our life for that matter, there are things that try to sidetrack us. Maybe you have tried before and can't seem to stick with it. Or you go for it with gusto for about a month, then lose interest, get too busy with other things, start doubting yourself, or whatever.

I have identified a few factors that are usually at work to try to stop us. I am sure there are more, but these are the ones I have seen most often. I call it the "SPIN Cycle." SPIN is an acronym for four behaviors that, in and of themselves, appear to be harmless and part of everyday life for most people.

- Stuck in the past

- Procrastination

- Internal negative thinking

- No clear vision

Stuck in the Past

I just mentioned that we can have a story from the past that continues to last. Going unchecked, past failures and hurts can keep us from moving forward. Failure is all in how you look at it. If you learn from it, then use what you learned as an educational process of what *not* to do in the future.

Remember, you can't change the past, but you can change the way it affects your present, and when you change your present, you are ultimately changing your future. Here are some symptoms that the past is still affecting you:

- You have feelings of revenge or can't get a past hurt out of your mind.

- You find yourself avoiding things you know you need to do.

- You tried once or twice and have not tried since.

- You are afraid of making mistakes or being rejected.

- You avoid trying new things.

Getting through past hurts and failures does not need to be a painful or long process. Once you recognize the behavior that tends to derail you, then you are more than half-way to recovery.

Therefore, if anyone is in Christ, he is a new creation; the
old has gone, the new has come! (2 Corinthians 5:17)

Maturing in your spiritual life does not happen instantly. As a matter of fact, it is a lifelong process. As we move closer to God's purposes, we sometimes feel guilty about how far from perfection we are compared to a perfect God. The key to breakthrough is to invite God into our imperfection. Instead of feeling guilty or thinking that you are a bad person, simply say to God, "This is me, your son/daughter, so please help me with this today." If you fall short, there is always forgiveness, and every day is a fresh new start.

Too often we allow feelings of failure to separate us from the life and love of God. He knows you more than you know yourself. He is not surprised when old behaviors and destructive patterns come up. When I read the Bible, I see many cases of imperfect people with a lot of issues who still did great things for God.

When the past comes knocking on your door, remember who you are now and who you are becoming through God! You can also do something practical to get through these past issues like call a friend, have someone pray with you, or talk with someone who can be an encouragement. Be sure to choose these people wisely.

There may be friends or family members who are not able to be a positive force in your life. Remember that Jesus was not honored or received well in His hometown of Galilee (see Matt. 6:4). There are people who may still see you as who you were in the past. Forgive them for not seeing you as you are today, and then identify positive, supportive "cheerleaders" that can help you break through when the past begins to hold you back.

Procrastination

Unfortunately, people procrastinate so much these days that they develop a lifestyle of avoidance instead of breaking through.

Procrastination is a lie that causes you to believe that avoiding something is somehow more beneficial than actually doing it. We all procrastinate to some degree. But procrastination is deadly when it becomes a lifestyle, because we can start to feel like we are a victim to our circumstances or to the demands of our daily lives.

Even while writing this section on procrastination, I was tempted to finish it later! But to prove that it is possible, I pushed through and finished this section even though it was inconvenient. There will always be things that will demand our time. A key to getting through this is to set priorities.

I usually begin my week by asking myself, what are one or two things that I need to get done this week that would most impact my life or projects. I write these down and schedule some time to work on them. Even if I don't have much time, I try to come up with one or two small steps I can take toward the task or major project that I am working on.

Most of the time, the reason we are putting things off is because the task or project may require a lot of time and effort. I used to think that to write a book I had to wait until I had a few weeks of undivided time to devote to writing, or at least a full day. Reality is that big blocks of time usually do not become available, and the result was that I could not finish a book.

I learned the breakthrough lifestyle of doing small things consistently. I now apply this to all the areas of my life. I write in my journal; I write blogs, articles, and small sections of book chapters on a daily basis. It does not seem like much at the time, but doing small things regularly produces results over time—and gets me through the lie that I don't have enough time.

Time is the one thing that we all have in common. It is something that we cannot get back and needs to be viewed as a gift. Developing yourself in any area you feel called to will help you. Think of it as working out physically or practicing a musical instrument. The more you do it, the more natural it will become.

Recognizing the problem of putting things off is a crucial step for recovery. I thought about writing a creative list of easy steps to get through the problem of procrastination. But if I lay it out too plain and simple, you might be tempted to procrastinate on doing the list.

Here's how most people ineffectively try to deal with procrastination:

You sit down and make a long list of everything you have been putting off for the past few years and prepare yourself to get it all done in one weekend. You remember that you need to *"seek first the Kingdom of God"* (Matt. 6:33) so you start out by praying—but the phone rings, so you answer it and talk with your friend about your list and ask that person to pray for you.

Back to the list. You pour yourself a cup of coffee and read the list over. Now you are really getting discouraged that your life is so out of control. So you have another cup of coffee and a cookie and get back to your list. You start to pray again, but you are interrupted by having to go to the bathroom again because you drank too much coffee.

Back to the list. You begin to cry and let it all out. Crying is good, right? Now you notice that the grout needs cleaned on your counter-top in the bathroom. At this point, scrubbing the grout sounds like more fun than your list.

Get back to your list. Oh, it is time to pray and give it all to God, but you are exhausted because it is your first day off in weeks. Since number one on your list is to get organized, you think that there might be a TV show on with organizational tips, so you grab a bag of chips and head for the couch!

Maybe that is an extreme example, but sometimes putting things off sounds like a lot more fun than doing it. The key is to not get overwhelmed:

- Break things down into small tasks.

- Find ways to do the small tasks over time.

- Learn to combine two things into one. If you want to pray and you need to exercise, then pray while you exercise.

My objective is to help you recognize that procrastination is a destiny killer. Learning to do small things over time is much easier to accomplish things you have been putting off.

Internal Negative Thinking

Your current life situation is a direct result of what you believe and do on a regular basis. The "I" in SPIN Cycle is for "internal negative thinking," or thoughts and beliefs that are often contrary to God's Word and His ways. God has great things in mind for all of us. His intention is that we succeed, prosper, and experience a life of love that bears real fruit—joy, peace, kindness, goodness, and more (see Gal. 5:22-23).

Past experiences or negative things spoken to us, particularly when we were young, can get embedded in our mind. We begin to believe these things even though they are not true. Phrases like, "You're stupid, you'll never make anything of yourself, you will not succeed, you don't deserve this…" are ungodly, disempowering beliefs. Unfortunately, many people have these small little thoughts that go undetected. They will pop up later on when we start to move toward our destiny or when good things begin to happen.

For the longest time, I seriously believed that I was not very smart. It held me back from going to college and stepping out in my gifts and talents. The strange thing about negative internal thinking is that usually people around you are telling you something opposite. For some reason, when we get these thoughts inside us, we can reject rational thinking.

The good news is that negative internal thinking can be changed around to be positive. This is the process of renewing our minds. The best way to break through this destructive pattern is to recognize your internal self-talk. Begin to notice what the voice inside your head is telling you. When you catch yourself thinking or saying something negative, turn it around and say or think the opposite. Begin to reinforce your new thinking on a regular basis. You may want to memorize some verses from the Bible that reveal the truth about who you really are through Christ (see, for example, 2 Cor. 5:17). Sometimes our biggest enemy is our own thoughts. These can be thoughts about ourselves, others, and God. God's love and power is unlimited. The only limits we have are what we believe about what we can do.

> *Therefore, prepare your minds for action; be self-controlled; set your hope fully on the grace to be given you when Jesus Christ is revealed* (1 Peter 1:13).

No Clear Vision

I meet and interact with a lot of people. I often ask what they want in life. Most people say, "I just want to be happy." When I ask them what happiness would look like, they don't know! If you are not clear about what it is you want, then how would you ever know if you have obtained it? This leads to living life with a cloudy vision. We will rarely make direct and focused decisions, often because we are afraid that we will make the wrong choices.

Clarity and focus causes us to become intentional. Something happens in the spiritual realm when we begin to pursue our life purpose. Clarity is actually linked with faith. Having faith is being certain or clear about God's desires for us. When we focus on God's intentions or will for our life, things are no longer cloudy. Our vision and destiny will become much clearer.

When you have a clear vision, then you begin to do things purposefully. You will move from the dissatisfaction of not knowing what to do to a passion for doing something. When you are clear about what you want, you can develop a plan to get to it. Obstacles are no longer viewed as setbacks because you will find a way to get through or go around them.

I know it sounds easy for me to say, "Just get a clear vision," but getting more focused at any level in your life is sure to help you. There will be times in your life when things are less clear than others. There are times when we are being tested by God to help us grow, and we need to press through the difficulty. Other times it is resistance from the enemy who does not want you to succeed. Or maybe you were never clear to begin with on what you wanted. The exercises you are doing in this book will help you with these areas.

> *If people can't see what God is doing, they stumble all over themselves; But when they attend to what he reveals, they are most blessed* (Proverbs 29:18 MSG).

Author K.L. Glanville was motivated to move forward with her plans to start a publishing business, and she published her first book, *The Realm: The Awakening Begins*, as a result of hearing this concept. In her words,

I had my iTunes set on shuffle with the option for about 600 songs. Within one week, Doug's audio message on "Getting Out of the SPIN Cycle" played several times. I had been kind of drifting with my direction, waiting for "something" to happen, but what really impacted me was that you don't need to sit around waiting for something new when God has already told you to do something. Another thing that's been helpful is the concept of doing "just one thing" every day. This took many of my overwhelming tasks and made them into bite-sized pieces, and allowed me to feel successful. I can encourage myself that I've done *something!*[2]

POSITIVE SPIN

If you have found yourself in the SPIN cycle, then the best thing to do is deal with any of the areas mentioned here. Here are a few ideas for getting get out of the negative SPIN cycle and move to a positive SPIN:

- **S**lingshot forward

- **P**roactive planning

- **I**ntentional action

- **N**o limits

Slingshot Forward

A good way to get focused is to do what I call the slingshot effect. This is where we pull back, or pull away for a while just like you would pull a slingshot back before it is propelled forward. Pulling back could be done in many different ways. Take time to pray specifically, and take time to listen to God for answers. Picture yourself in the slingshot and God's hand safely holding you. Try taking a weekend away or take walks or long drives, and focus on where you are and where you feel God is calling you to be.

I went through a three-year process in the sling when I moved from Los Angeles, California, to Moravian Falls, North Carolina. I am more of a big city guy who likes being around action and fun. My wife and I felt that God was directing us to go buy a cabin in the foothills of the Appalachian Mountains. It was not our style, and the nearest Starbucks was over an hour away!

During that time, I still traveled and spoke at conferences, but when I came home I was in a peaceful environment that forced me into a new lifestyle that I was not able to experience in Los Angeles. I wrote the majority of this book during that time in the sling before God's "slingshot" released and sent me back to the West Coast. You don't have to move to the mountains; you can do this in your own community. Take time to pray and ask God for new direction.

Proactive Planning

Whether you are waiting for God to give you direction or you know what you want to do and you need some details to get there, it is good to be proactive about it. The Merriam-Webster dictionary defines *proactive* as "acting in anticipation of future problems, needs, or changes."[3] When you want to move toward your destiny and purpose in life, it is good to begin to anticipate what you will need for the future.

For instance, if you feel that God is directing you toward starting a business, but you don't have a lot of clarity on the entire process, then you can be proactive by doing some research, taking classes, or talking with others who have gone through the process. Praying specifically can be a way to be proactive.

Intentional Action

Being intentional may sound similar to proactive, but being proactive deals more with preparing for the future, whereas being intentional is something you can do daily toward what you feel called to do. Being intentional gets you out of your comfort zone and causes you to take steps that you normally may not do. If you find yourself in a negative SPIN, then you can take intentional steps to get out instead of just waiting for it to blow over or stop on its own. Most people are waiting for God to strike them with a lightning bolt or speak audibly about their destiny. You can do things now that will build the foundation inside you and train you for later events.

I got a phone call a while back from a man who wanted to do some of the same types of things that I am doing with public speaking and coaching. He was very early in his process, but wanted help with finding some steps he could take that would prepare him while he was waiting on God to open opportunities at a greater level. Making the phone call to me and asking was being intentional.

No Limits

The way to get out of a negative SPIN and the quickest way to get to your destiny is to realize that there are no limits to what you can do through God's unlimited power and love! It is amazing what we can do when we tap into the principles of the Bible along with the power of the Holy Spirit.

This was a tough concept for me to grasp. Years ago, I knew I was called to something bigger, but I kept thinking that I would accomplish it with my current understanding and experience. When

I tapped into the unlimited power of God and began to be proactive and intentional, I was amazed by how things began to happen!

My wife used to tell me years ago that I needed to be mentored by someone in a higher-level position of what I felt called to do. I could not comprehend how I would get close to someone at that level. Through a series of events, I had the opportunity to become a Web master and technical coordinator for an international ministry. As a result, I ended up becoming one of the speakers for this organization and I was personally mentored by the founder. This was one more major step in helping me achieve my destiny of having my own ministry that helps others.

> *No eye has seen, no ear has heard, no mind has conceived what God has prepared for those who love him* (1 Corinthians 2:9).

As long as we are putting our relationship with God first in our lives and growing in maturity, then you can bet that God will open greater opportunities for us.

> *...Everything is possible for him who believes* (Mark 9:23).

> *Commit to the Lord whatever you do, and your plans will succeed* (Proverbs 16:3).

EXERCISE: GETTING OUT OF THE SPIN CYCLE

Maybe you have already developed a breakthrough lifestyle and you are looking for some tools to get you to the next level. If are not there yet, then it is good to recognize the things that trip you up most often when it comes to moving toward your destiny.

1. Similar to the exercise we did in Chapter 1, what is one decision or task that you have been putting off, that if you did it would change your life in some way?

2. Think about the SPIN cycle and try to identify the destructive behavior that holds you back from doing it.

   - Stuck in the past

   - Procrastination

   - Internal negative thinking

   - No clear vision

3. Instead of focusing on the negative SPIN, which will probably discourage you, let's jump to the positive SPIN.

   - Slingshot forward—Go for a walk or drive and ask God to speak to you about why you would be avoiding anything in your life that would be good for you to do. Write down what you sense God telling you.

- Proactive planning—What is a step you can take toward the decision or task you need to do? Be sure to do it today.

- Intentional action—Make a commitment once a week to identify something you are putting off, and take a step toward doing it. This might be taking another step toward a decision you made previously.

- No limits—With God, all things are possible. Pray and begin to think about some of the bigger things you want to do in life. We'll do another exercise later to identify them.

By doing these steps regularly, you will eventually develop a habit of breaking through instead of putting off.

You can go to www.personaldevelopmentgodsway.com to download the exercise so that you can do it on your computer.

ENDNOTES

1. Joey Green, *The Road to Success Was Paved With Failure* (Joey Green, 2001), back cover.

2. K.L. Glanville, *The Realm: The Awakening Begins* (Monterey Park, CA: Luminations Media Group, Inc., 2008).

3. In *Merriam-Webster Online Dictionary*. Retrieved December 21, 2009, from http://www.merriam-webster.com/dictionary/proactive.

Chapter 7

RADICAL CHANGE

UNDERSTANDING CHANGE

Have you ever felt as though your brain was going to explode with too much information? Sometimes reading a book like this is like trying to take a drink of water from a fire hydrant. One little sip is what you thought you would get, but instead you get a seemingly overwhelming blast of knowledge.

Making personal change is not always easy, especially since we live in a stressed-out world that is on information-overload. The last thing we need is more information and one more thing to do. Because of world-shaking tragedies and terrorism, people today can easily feel out of control and disempowered to do anything about it. In response, it is common for people to keep a sense of stability in their lives through routine and predictability.

We all have different personality styles. Some people enjoy change, but the vast majority of people avoid it by nature. My hunch is that you would not be reading this book if you did not want to change something in your life. Let's go deeper into this subject of how to radically revolutionize your life.

The definition of change is to cause to be different, or to transform from one thing to another. A biblical understanding of change is getting to know God's will, and in the process we begin to transform or renew our minds. One thing is certain: God does not change. We can trust and find stability in God's love for us.

> *Every good and perfect gift is from above, coming down from the Father of the heavenly lights, who does not change like shifting shadows* (James 1:17).

> *Jesus Christ is the same yesterday and today and forever* (Hebrews 13:8).

God does not change, but He does bring about new things continually. He wants us to be renewed over and over.

> *See, I am doing a new thing! Now it springs up; do you not perceive it? I am making a way in the desert and streams in the wasteland* (Isaiah 43:19).

People ask, "How do I know God's will for my life?" Well, Romans 12:2 is pretty clear: You start by transforming your thinking away from the pattern of the world, or logic, into the unlimited possibilities of God's power and love.

> *Do not conform any longer to the pattern of this world, but be transformed by the renewing of your mind. Then you will be able to test and approve what God's will is—his good, pleasing and perfect will* (Romans 12:2).

Change is inevitable. Everything is changing on a regular basis. Computers get faster and smaller; there are new records to beat for athletes; with each new invention comes more possibilities.

Change is also necessary. If we don't ever experience change in our lives, we can become stagnant and bored. If we are not challenged to improve, no matter what age we are, we become weakened and vulnerable.

People don't gravitate toward change because we like certainty, and change involves facing the unknown. Change can be painful, and we like pleasurable experiences. Change requires effort, and most of us already have too much to do.

Positive change is not automatic, but requires an intentional effort on our part. Remember that some people are motivated to do something because they have passion and are excited about it. You may not have this drive, but maybe you are dissatisfied with an area of your life right now.

Whether your motivation to change is from a passion change in your life, or from dissatisfaction with your life, you can use this motivation to create a *transformed* life.

No matter what has happened in the past or how many times you have tried and failed, today is a fresh new start. Every day is a new chance! By now you can see that if you change the way you view things, you can break through whatever has held you back in the past.

WHAT ARE YOU FOCUSING ON?

How you view a situation is vital. If you continually focus on what is wrong or the reasons why you can't do something, you will eventually convince yourself that you can't change the situation, whether it is based on fact or not. There is a spiritual principle that what you focus on continually eventually comes to you.

If you search for good, you will find favor; but if you search for evil, it will find you! (Proverbs 11:27 NLT)

We can create self-fulfilling prophecies about ourselves and our situation based on what we focus on. You may not be seeking evil intent, but this verse in Proverbs shows that you get what you search for or put your energy into. If you continually think that you are a failure, then you probably fail often, at least in your own mind.

I enjoy comedy so several years ago I got trained and began to incorporate stand-up comedy into my ministry. Laughter is like medicine to the soul. One of my first really big gigs was sold out with over 300 people and two other professional comedians. Somehow I was the headliner and had to do 45 minutes of material! I was prepared, but after sitting in the crowd listening to the other comedians, I suddenly was hit with doubt, and I started thinking that I was not all that good at comedy. I was convinced that I would flop pretty badly. As I did my portion of the show, there were lots of laughs, but since I had already convinced myself I would fail, I thought they were courtesy laughs from people feeling sorry for me. Later, I found out that the other two comedians were very impressed, and I watched the video and was laughing very hard and thought I did great. The moral of that story is to not believe the negative things that pop into our minds. These thoughts of failure can cause us to think we failed, when in fact we have not.

For as he thinks in his heart, so is he (Proverbs 23:7 NKJV).

We can derail our destiny by focusing on negative things. We also can get weighed down with emotional baggage that we may not know is there. For instance, if you have a large amount of debt and you are continually thinking about how bad being in debt feels, most likely you will carry the stress of the situation with you through your entire life. It is like a weight around your neck and shoulders of shame and even hopelessness.

A solution is to decide right now that you will put a debt reduction plan in place and get on with life. Place the feelings of failure and shame in God's hands, and begin to put your thoughts and energy into finding creative ways to earn additional money and have fun in the process and you will have instant change!

Have you ever thought someone did something wrong to you? Did you get angry and hurt, only to find out that the person had no bad intentions at all? What happened to your hurt and anger? It went away immediately because you were no longer focused on it, and you got a new perspective. We can train ourselves to get a new perspective on everything that happens to us.

There was a time in my life that whenever something bad happened to me I blamed it on God, and I would get so angry. Then one day I realized that it was not God's nature to cause bad things to happen. My view of God changed instantly because I changed my focus and perspective. Then I realized that stuff happens in life, but I don't have to let it crush me.

You can actually stop in the midst of a bad day and change the way you view it. Your attitude and emotions can positively change in a heartbeat. I remember driving to work with a busy day ahead of me. When I arrived, I realized that I forgot my parking garage key-card at home. I was already running late and feeling very frustrated. I had to drive back home and get the key-card, adding an hour to my commute in Los Angeles. I decided to apply this principle and changed my focus instantly by saying, "Thank You, God, for giving me extra time in the car to pray and listen to an encouraging audio message." I turned a bad day into a good one. By the time I arrived back at the office, I had more peace than normal, and people took notice.

> *Where your focus goes, your energy flows.*

Learning to change your perspective is a step toward renewing your mind as mentioned in Romans 12:2. We can choose to focus on good things, and if we do this regularly, our outlook on life will change dramatically. We will begin to see the positive in the midst of difficulty.

Decide ahead of time what you are going to focus on. With just a small amount of effort, you can learn to turn bad situations in to good ones. You can learn to make the most of every situation. It is not worth getting upset! Some people say life is too short to be upset or angry. I have always thought that life is too long to do it as well.

PAIN VERSUS PLEASURE—MAKING THINGS FUN

If we want to bring radical change, there is a chance that we might have areas of our lives in which we are limiting ourselves. Interestingly, most limitations are self-imposed. What you believe about yourself and the world around you can either keep you locked behind your fears or thrust you forward into living your dreams.

Let's look at one of the primary drivers of internal thinking. I made a considerable amount of progress in my own life when I discovered that nearly everything we do is motivated by the desire to avoid painful experiences, and that we naturally gravitate toward things that make us feel good.

This concept is found in the *pain versus pleasure* principle, a psychology term made popular by Sigmund Freud. Take a closer look, though, and you will find that this concept was actually borrowed from the Bible. Pain versus pleasure may sound strange for some of you, but human nature causes us to avoid things that are uncomfortable and gravitate toward things that feel good, whether they are good for us or not. Procrastination is a good example of how this principle works.

Whenever we procrastinate, it's because deep down we believe that avoiding the situation will make us feel better than actually doing it, as discussed in the last chapter.

To break through, we must turn this around and realize that avoiding will actually bring greater pain in the long run than if we take care of it today. We avoid things because we view them as painful to some degree. If this was not true, then we would do it immediately. We need to be willing to face reality and see the future results of our avoidance. When we can see what will happen if we continue to avoid the situation, it will give us the extra push we need to get it done.

If we develop a lifestyle of avoiding, we begin to believe that the small amount of pleasure we are gaining by not doing a task is somehow better than the pain of doing it. At any given moment, our reality is based on what we focus on. If we focus on the painful aspect of a task, then we will feel discouraged. Remember that redirecting what you focus on will allow you to do things that bring radical change relatively fast.

If you are constantly focusing on the pain it takes to do something, you will be discouraged. Instead, focus on the good and pleasurable results you will have if you take steps to accomplish the task. This lifestyle of avoidance has led many of us to associate a great amount of pleasure with doing things that are not good for us, like overeating. Quite often, the things that are not good for us are the things we actually gravitate toward. We must change the way we associate pain and pleasure in order to change our behavior.

Here are two examples of this principle from the Bible:

In Acts 9:1-18, the apostle Paul (who was named Saul at the time) converted to Christianity during a radical encounter with Jesus on his journey to the city of Damascus. God sent a man named Ananias to tell him that he was called to suffer for Christ. As Saul began to preach the Good News of Jesus, he was opposed and even had threats against his life. Instead of facing the suffering (which he was ultimately called to do), he ran, and in Damascus he was lowered in a basket through a hole in the wall. Later he admitted that this was weakness on his part (see 2 Cor. 11:30-33). It was not until Paul changed his view—and considered suffering and affliction for Christ to be "glory beyond comparison" (see 2 Cor. 4:16-18) that he went from being a frightened evangelist to a bold apostle.

Paul changed his negative focus that to suffer for Christ was a frightening thing to a new way of thinking. In his new focus, he believed that suffering for Christ was not only good, it was an important part of God's will for his life. He reassociated what it meant to suffer with something good, and after that he was able to endure suffering and persecution beyond imagining. The more suffering he experienced, the more glory of God he would encounter, and he became unstoppable.

Another example of changed focus is found the night before Jesus was crucified, when He went to the Garden of Gethsemane to pray. He clearly was having a difficult time and did not want to go through with the task before Him. He asked God to remove this painful assignment from him. He had to come to the point where He realized that there was much more to gain through his suffering than if He did not do it. That is when he finally said, *"Not My will but Your will be done"* (Luke 22:42).

We make associations all the time. Have you ever gotten sick on a certain food, and then when you smell the food years later you still feel ill? Maybe you listened to a song while you were sad, and to this day when you hear that song it brings the sadness back as if it was yesterday. Negative associations like these can bring fear and doubt and cause us to pull back instead of moving forward. Recognizing them will help us break through some of the covert roadblocks to our destiny.

Let's look at how this principle can affect relationships. Maybe you believe that being in a relationship will bring you great satisfaction. But based on past experiences, you have associated that being in a relationship is painful. So when things begin to go well, you may begin to find fault in the other person and subconsciously sabotage the relationship so you can feel the pain you think should be in a relationship. Reality is that relationships all have some pain, but true love brings a satisfaction that is beyond compare. You'll need to reassociate being in a relationship with the good benefits as opposed to your bad experiences.

This principle can have a staggering effect on success. Say that you really have a desire to succeed and find great satisfaction in owning your own business. But in the back of your mind you have a belief that success will bring big headaches, more taxes, and employee problems. You have given up in the past because of the stress; then when you get to a certain place of succeeding you will most likely sabotage your success in some way. You might disconnect, avoid making decisions, find yourself drawn to old addictions, and so on.

Again, there is a need to reassociate the good benefits of success and see that they outweigh the pain of common business problems. Then you will be more willing to break through and not give up when times get difficult. These patterns are real and are alive and active in each of us to some degree. You can break through them by changing what kinds of things you associate with pain and pleasure.

Here's what I discovered about myself. For nearly three years I knew that God was calling me to write a book. I was a successful conference speaker and my schedule was filled a year in advance. I developed a message that was helping thousands of people find new creative ways to share God's love. I had done all the research for a new book idea and even road-tested my ideas by doing outreach events for several years so I knew that it worked. People everywhere were telling me they wanted to read my book once I wrote it.

So what was stopping me? Though I was not consciously aware of it, I determined that I had fear of failure. It was so painful every time I sat down to write, because I had never written a book before and was never that good at English class in school. I had thoughts of the book turning out really bad and people not liking it. I also had to submit it to a publisher and it was going to be read by many of my colleagues and friends that I highly respect.

However, what if I did not write it and later in life I realized that I missed a great opportunity? What if someone else wrote a book similar to mine and it was successful? If I did write it, possibly tens of thousands of people all over the world could read it and be changed. I would begin to generate revenue from the sales that would allow me to do more events and impact even more people. The fact was that I would experience much more gain by writing it than not writing it. I had to come to a place where I realized that *not* writing my book was actually more painful than the pain of writing it.

OK, now I was convinced. However, writing it was still very hard for me. I needed to find a way to make this painful process enjoyable and fun. Even though I do not drink much coffee, I really love going to places like Starbucks and hanging out at coffeehouses where I feel really inspired. So I went to Starbucks every day, and within three weeks I had written the initial manuscript. I have to admit my rear was a bit sore from those wooden chairs, but I found a way to make writing fun. I listened to music during the process and got to know other people who were there writing, too. We encouraged each other.

As it turned out, the book I wrote, *Prophecy, Dreams, and Evangelism*, was liked by thousands of people, and I am so glad I broke through. Now I love to write, and it is not a painful process at all. Since then, I write almost on a daily basis. My fear was holding me back from a gift that I was not aware I had.

I have gotten dozens of e-mails from people who have heard me talk about this and have written their book in a matter of weeks. If you want to break through and accomplish the things you want in life, you must follow through and find out what it is that is stopping you.

So to recap, you can actually change instantly by choosing what you will focus on and how you will view a situation. You can find ways to get yourself to break through any situation by recognizing the reason you are putting it off or avoiding doing what you need to do. Difficult tasks can weigh us down even more with the pain we have subconsciously associated with them. If we recognize the pain and find a way to make it fun, or find a big enough reason to follow through, nothing can hold us back!

EXERCISE: PAIN AND PLEASURE PRINCIPLE IN YOUR LIFE

You may not realize that the steps that hold people back the most in going for their destiny is simply learning to do things, make decisions, and follow though. This is what will set you apart and cause you to begin working hand in hand with God, moving toward what you feel called to do. It is not just about doing things you put off; it is finding a way to make it fun and make it happen without having to consciously think about it.

1. Let's take a look at one of the things that you have been putting off that you listed in the exercise in Chapter 1 or in the last chapter.

2. Think about the pain and pleasure principle, and write down any pain you have associated with each of the tasks you were putting off.

3. Write down the pleasure you have gained by not doing the tasks you are putting off. Maybe you have more time because you don't have to do the steps to move forward, you can eat anything, etc. You get my drift.

4. Write a few sentences about what it will cost you if you do not follow through. What will you miss? How will you feel? What will happen?

5. Begin to associate something good (pleasure) with following through on the tasks. What benefits will

you gain? What positive things will happen? How could you make it fun?

You can go to www.personaldevelopmentgodsway.com to download the exercise so that you can do it on your computer.

Chapter 8

PERSONAL TRANSFORMATION

DESIGNING YOUR LIFE

Depending on your personality style, you are either drawn to the idea of life planning, or it may make you feel restricted. We are all wired differently, so I like to think of the process in a more creative light, like designing your life instead of planning. Planning sounds like it is set in stone, whereas designing is more organic and allows you to be creative as you go. Consider what Jesus says about planning in Luke 14:28. Counting the cost is the same as creating a plan.

> *Suppose one of you wants to build a tower. Will he not first sit down and estimate the cost to see if he has enough money to complete it?* (Luke 14:28)

In Matthew 25:14-30, Jesus tells a parable of a land owner who gave one man approximately $5,000, another $2,000, and another guy $1,000. The ones who received $2,000 and $5,000 were able to double their money by taking some steps to put it to work. But the man who was given $1,000 buried it in the ground and did nothing to increase his money. The owner was not happy with the man who did nothing. That parable was given to us to show us that we are all given gifts and talents from God "according to our abilities," and He really wants us to use them.

Unfortunately, some people don't see the value of improving themselves because they don't see the direct link between their behavior and God's gifts and destiny in life. You are God's divine creation. Imagine the possibilities if Christians began using the God-given biblical principles we have been discussing. Many people would find their destiny and improve their lives through the empowerment of the Holy Spirit. Churches would find creative ways to fund ministry projects, families would be strengthened, our children would step into their destines at a young age, and we could all become, once again, the greatest example of God's power on earth.

OVERCOMING FEAR

Why are not more people cashing in on all that God has for them? A major reason is fear. A quick way to overcome fear is the power of focus that we discussed in previous chapters. Remember that whatever we focus on becomes our reality, whether it is rational or reality or not. If we focus on why we cannot do something, we will never be able to do it. You might be focusing too much on how hard it is to change, instead of focusing on how easy it is to take small steps each day.

Fear of rejection, fear of failure, fear of success, fear of being alone, fear of love, fear of the unknown—whatever it might be for you, it boils down to not being good for you. Fear is one of the biggest things that will stop you from moving forward and doing the things that will get you to your destiny. The words "do not be afraid" appear in the Bible nearly 70 times. That's a lot.

> *But now, this is what the Lord says—…"Fear not, for I have redeemed you; I have summoned you by name; you are mine. When you pass through the waters, I will be with you; and when you pass through the rivers, they will not sweep over you. When you walk through the fire, you will not be burned; the flames will not set you ablaze* (Isaiah 43:1-2).

The best way to deal with fear is to recognize it for what it is and move forward. The Bible tells us that fear is not just an emotion, but can be a spirit as well. It is important to give all of our fear over to God and ask Him to give us a "sound mind" to recognize it for what it is.

> *For God has not given us a spirit of fear, but of power and of love and of a sound mind* (2 Timothy 1:7 NKJV).

Sometimes we don't move forward into our destiny, or we are not able to change, because we don't know what we want. But when you know what you want and you are not able to break through or follow through, then what's really stopping you may be fear.

KEYS TO OVERCOMING FEAR

Have you ever been afraid and you could feel the adrenalin rush inside you? Fear can be like energy that sweeps over you physically. It is possible, then, to redirect it and let it propel you into action instead of moving away from it. Instead of letting it control you, simply admit it is scary and redirect the energy to move through it.

Most of the time it takes more energy to fight the fear than it does to face it down.

Can you remember the first time you jumped off a diving board into deep water? How did you do it? I yelled the entire way! What people did not know is that I could not swim, but I learned to swim really quickly after I hit the water. I remember looking over the edge into the water and I was paralyzed, but my friends cheered me on. After I did it a couple of times, the fear left. As you press through, you will find that the situation becomes less and less scary. If you do this on a regular basis, you will learn a new habit of breaking through.

I used to be dreadfully afraid of public speaking. After putting myself in a position to do it a few times, I was able to break through this fear, and I now do it for a living and love it. Take some practical steps to get through your fear: take a public speaking class, speak in a small group, make the phone call you need to make, get the application for school, or whatever. Take a step today!

I used to be afraid of flying. It was the turbulence I did not like. I was terrified. Then my job required me to fly a lot. I read a book on the fear of flying and realized that most of my fear was not based on fact. I now help other people around me on the plane when things get rough. I usually tell people that we would pay good money at Disneyland for this kind of ride, and I throw my hands up like we are on a roller coaster. Just joking usually helps people break from their fears enough to realize that there are thousands of flights a day and the chance of crash is not likely. The power of focus can help you gain a new perspective on anything you fear.

Karen knew that God was calling her to lead Bible studies and small group discussions at her church. She was so afraid of speaking even in front of a small group of friends. She bravely took a practical step by taking a public speaking class at a community college, where she blasted through her fears by giving a speech in front of the class. After doing this several times, she is not only leading her small Bible study group; she has been able to speak at the evening meetings at her church in front of many people, and she really enjoys it.

Dying to Yourself

When we think of breaking through our fears, some people would rather die! Seriously, some people dread things like public speaking more than death. A key element to renewing our minds and transforming our character to be more like Christ is a process that the Bible calls sanctification. It requires us to "die to ourselves" and allow God's Spirit to live through us.

There are several verses in the Bible that talk about dying to our sinful nature, or "old self," and allowing God to live in us.

> *For we know that our old self was crucified with him so that the body of sin might be done away with, that we should no longer be slaves to sin—because anyone who has died has been freed from sin* (Romans 6:6-7).

> *I have been crucified with Christ and I no longer live, but Christ lives in me. The life I live in the body, I live by faith in the Son of God, who loved me and gave himself for me* (Galatians 2:20).

This is a necessary process for transforming your life. However, it is also a very misunderstood principle, and many people take this to the extreme and believe that they must die to all desires and plans that they have. It does not mean that we cannot have any desires or ideas of our own. If that were the case, you would become an android for God. God wants to give us good things that we desire and would enjoy.

> *Delight yourself in the Lord and he will give you the desires of your heart* (Psalm 37:4).

Dying to yourself means that you have renewed your life through God's Holy Spirit and you now have the right motives and intentions in things that you do. The meaning of the verse isn't that you can't have a desire or ambition of your own; it means that once you have purified motives, God actually wants to give you your desires. You must allow God to change your character and motives, so that you will not go after things with greed and lust for your own power and promotion.

I like to think of this concept as holding two glasses of water, one in your right hand and one in your left. The one in your right hand represents all your experiences and the water in that glass is half full, murky, and unclear. It contains some good things but also some not so good qualities and bad experiences. The glass in your left hand represents the pure wisdom and character of God. It is full and crystal clear.

Most people think that, to get more of God into your life, you simply pour the water from His glass into yours, in a sense getting filled up with more of God. That will still produce murky, unclear water. You must first empty your glass, wipe it out, and then fill it with God's pure living water. This is a process of becoming pure, holy, or more like Christ and an analogy of sanctification. This is why Jesus refers to himself as Living Water that will cause you to never (spiritually) thirst again (see John 4:10-11).

For example, let's say that having wealth can be a good desire and destiny for your life. But if your desire to be rich is rooted in motives of greed, lust, and pride, the water in your glass (your heart) will be murky and unclear. It will be unhealthy for you to drink. You can choose to allow these motivations to die and let God's character and motivations of generosity, love, and humility clean your heart (your glass) and fill you with clear, clean "living water." This water is not only healthy for you to drink, but you can share it with others and never run out!

There is a lot of preaching and talking about renewing your mind, but I have found very little practical instruction on how to really do it. It is not always as easy as thinking positive things or reciting Bible verses, though these things are good. I did this for years, yet was not able to get rid of lustful thoughts. The more I tried *not* to think about not thinking about it, the more I thought about it. Instead, I had to stop myself from focusing on the negative things that pulled me down, by replacing them with thoughts of being thankful for God's continual grace that is available to me. Eventually, the thoughts began losing their power because I was spending my energy more on focusing on God's love and grace. I would pray, "God, I am thankful for Your continual grace to change my thoughts to Your thoughts, my vision to Your vision."

To transform your mind and change the way you think often requires changing things that drive your thoughts at a subconscious level. Advertising and commercials are already doing this to us, so why not find a way to do it for ourselves in a positive way?

Transform Your Thinking

It is hard to keep asking yourself to not think a thought, but it is easy to give yourself something good to think about instead. It is hard to focus on not doing something, but it is easier to focus on taking a positive action. When we grasp this, we are no longer struggling and beating ourselves up for thinking and doing things that are not good for us.

Renewing your mind and developing godly character involves more than trying to avoid sin. If you continually focus on what you are not supposed to do, or on the negative thoughts or behaviors, then that is all you will be thinking about all the time. Eventually you will feel guilty for not being able to change. In the New Testament, Peter instructs us to set the focus of our minds on the positive things that are coming as opposed to negative thoughts.

> *Therefore, prepare your minds for action; be self-controlled; set your hope fully on the grace to be given you when Jesus Christ is revealed* (1 Peter 1:13).

Most people are not aware of the fact that our brain is not able to deal with the words like "no" or "do not." When we are told to not think about something, we cannot help thinking about it. If I tell you right now, "Don't think of a pink elephant—don't do it!" You can't help thinking of a pink elephant, because in order to understand what I just said, your brain had to process the command and think of the very thing I told you not to think of.

How about a father saying to his daughter who is wearing a new white blouse, "Whatever you do, don't spill your chocolate milk." You guessed it, she spilled the milk. She was not even thinking of spilling it until the idea of spilling it was introduced into her mind as a possibility. It would have made more sense for this father to say, "You are doing a great job drinking your milk," which would encourage her to not spill it. This could be why in the Bible you will read more about what you should do as opposed to what you should not. Yes, there are some don'ts in there, but you will find more do's than don'ts.

Remember the power of focus. If we are focusing on the negative, we will continually have to deal with negative things. Continual focus on resisting only causes the negative thoughts to persist.

Instead, redirect your thoughts to something good, like Peter said, "Think about the grace that will be given to you." I find this to be much more productive.

> *I get better results in my own life if I focus more on what I should do as opposed to what I should not.*

The apostle Paul mentions the same principle:

Finally, brothers, whatever is true, whatever is noble, whatever is right, whatever is pure, whatever is lovely, whatever is admirable—if anything is excellent or praiseworthy—think about such things (Philippians 4:8).

Paul also talks about developing the fruit (or evidence) of the Spirit in us: love, joy, peace, patience, kindness, goodness, faithfulness, gentleness, and self-control (see Galatians 5:22-23). Peter wrote about how to develop a divine nature. He said to add these qualities—goodness, knowledge, self-control, perseverance, godliness, brotherly kindness, and love—one on top of another, to build our faith (see 2 Peter 1:5-7).

It will take practice to renew your mind and begin to change your character to be more like God's. Notice that Paul refers to character as fruit, which implies that it does not happen overnight, but there is a growth process involved. You may want to do what I did. I memorized the fruit of the Spirit in Galatians 5:22-23, and I say them in my mind as I walk throughout the day. Several times a day, with each step, I say each of the fruits to get them into my spirit and my mind. Since I do it while walking and praying, my body and spirit are involved as well. After a few weeks, I found myself thinking of these qualities automatically while I walked. I had begun to automatically respond to these godly characteristics without having to consciously think of them.

Believe It or Not—It's Probably Your Belief System

I have been in the process of transformation for a couple of decades. I noticed that when things started to go well for me, all of a sudden something would happen, and I would mess up, or I would slip back to my old ways. Has this ever happened to you? Things start going well, and you are becoming more successful, when out of the blue you are tempted with old destructive behaviors. You start getting stressed from overwork and run yourself down. In this weakened state, you're more prone to give in and jeopardize all that you have worked for.

People usually chalk this up to spiritual warfare, which it could very well be. However, if it happens repeatedly, there is a good chance that a subconscious behavior is influencing you. Remember the breaker switch analogy from earlier? It is most likely from your own beliefs, because what we believe about ourselves and about God can influence our behavior. Yes, satan might be attacking you, but he might be using your own beliefs to do it. He tried this with Jesus in the wilderness by using verses out of context to try to tempt Him. The verses from the Torah were part of Jesus' beliefs, but satan twisted them.

We all develop a belief system at a very young age. A belief system is the way we think things "should be" that defines our worldview and what we value. Most of our beliefs are not usually based on reality or something we thought through and wisely chose. Studies indicate that over 80 percent of our beliefs were learned before age 8. Most everything we do is motivated from our subconscious belief systems.

Beliefs motivated by fear and doubt can act as a thermostat. When things start to heat up in your life and the atmosphere begins to change for the good, you subconsciously "kick on the air conditioner." Fear and doubt make you want to bring things back down to a level that feels more comfortable; to a place where you think you should be. In many cases, these beliefs cause us to think much less of ourselves than what God thinks of us. Remember, God sees you in your full potential.

Beliefs that cause us to pull back can be why relationships fail, people have affairs, overeat, and use alcohol or drugs. The widespread addiction to pornography can be partially attributed to people self-sabotaging their destinies without consciously knowing why. Unless you have gone through a belief system assessment, you are probably operating with a belief system that you did not choose, but was developed and influenced by others: maybe your parents, teachers, or friends. I don't want to dishonor parents or teachers. They most likely did not choose their belief system, either, and they simply passed on someone else's to you.

Growing up, you may have heard things like:

- Who do you think you are?

- Money does not grow on trees.

- You are not as pretty as your sister.

- You will never make anything of yourself.

- Why don't you get a real job?

- You're a loser.

- You're just like your father.

- I'm ashamed of you.

- When are you going to grow up?

- You make me sick.

These types of statements get ingrained in you. At a young age you can start believing them even though they are not true. Your brain is like a computer. It gets programmed by experiences. These programs run in the background and pop thoughts into your head that negatively influence your self-image. The sad part is that someone said the same things to the person who said these things to you. It gets passed down from generation to generation.

We can also have godly beliefs: good things that come from the process of renewing your mind through the power of the Spirit. Godly beliefs empower us. They can come from someone in authority affirming us at a young age.

We can also have ungodly beliefs: old negative thoughts about ourselves, others, and life in general. Ungodly beliefs limit and weaken us. They cause us to have a dim outlook on life, low self-esteem, and even depression. An effective and practical way to quickly renew your mind is to identify and change beliefs that are not good for you. Remember that you have the power to choose, and you can get out of limiting behavior and thinking.

Any time an embedded belief conflicts with a situation in our life, we will experience some type of discomfort: stress, frustration, anger, fear, and so on. Pain and conflict can be indicators that we either need to change the situation or our belief about it. Again, the way we view things can make or break us.

EXAMPLES OF BELIEFS AND SITUATIONS IN CONFLICT

- You developed a belief when you were young that you should read the Bible and pray every day to be a good Christian. Your life situation is now very busy, and you don't always get to it. The result is that you feel guilty, which is uncomfortable. Your options to resolve this can include that you change the way you use your time and set aside some time to read the Bible, or change your belief and know that God loves you whether you read the Bible daily or not. I recommend reading it, but don't beat yourself up over it.

- You developed a belief from your parents that you should make a good living to be a good father or mother. But in your current life situation you don't make that much money and sometimes change jobs a lot. The result is that you feel like a failure inside, which is uncomfortable. Solution, you can change to a job that better suits you, or change this belief and realize that loving your family and building strong relationships makes you a good parent and spouse, not your job and how much money you make.

- You have always believed and your friends tell you that you should get married to be happy, but you can't seem to find the right person. When you find someone that might be "the one," the relationship seems to break up without your knowing exactly why. The result is that you feel unfulfilled and very unhappy, which is uncomfortable. Solution, you can break through and believe that you will find the right person, find out the root cause of destructive relational behavior, or change that original belief so that you are happy whether you are married or not.

The solutions in these examples are far from complete but are given to present a few examples of how belief systems can work in your life. You can change the situation or simply change the belief. Let's say you have a job that you like, but you don't like your boss. You can either change jobs, or pray and ask God to give you grace to get along with your boss. The key is to get rid of the negative feelings that cause you stress and feelings of avoidance. We still want to be sensitive to the Holy Spirit convicting us of things we need to change, but there is a big difference between conviction from God and condemnation and guilt from ourselves.

We really don't have time to go into this in detail, but it would be beneficial for you to pray about this and consider if you have any beliefs that are ungodly or in conflict with your current situation. An easy way to do this is to ask God to show you any ungodly beliefs that have been limiting you and write them down. These are usually things like, "I will never change, I cannot be successful, I can never love again, I cannot make decisions, I am not able to be wealthy, I am always depressed, and so on."

Believing these things has cost you something in your life. They have robbed you of peace, caused undue stress, and even stopped you from moving forward. If you believe that you will never change, then it may have caused you to stay in a rut. You may have missed opportunities to advance by believing these lies about yourself. Pray and ask God to turn these negative beliefs around and give you new positive beliefs about who you are. It is good to remember who we are in Christ. I go into more detail about changing your beliefs at some of my live events.

WHO I AM IN CHRIST

Here is the *truth* about who we are in Christ. You can say it as a prayer:

In Christ, I am a new creation, and all the old thoughts and behaviors no longer have power over me. I am being renewed every day with God's love and character. I share in God's divine nature because God's Spirit lives in me. I am free from condemnation and have the strength to live my life free of negative thoughts and desires of my flesh. I am God's workmanship, created to do good works, which God has prepared for me ahead of time to accomplish. I am more than a conqueror through God who loves me. I have a clear mind and can make good decisions. I am increasing daily in faith, strength, wisdom, and love. I am able to love others because God has first loved me.

EXERCISE: SEEING WHO YOU ARE BECOMING

You probably have already had some sense or glimpse of what you would like to do or be in the future. You have learned that God sees you and relates to you according to who you are becoming, and He will help you to get there. In this exercise you are going to practice seeing yourself that way.

We are going to pretend for a moment that you already know what you are destined to do in life. Pretend you are in the future, and money is no object. In this exercise you are being asked to list as many things as you can on a separate piece of paper or on your computer of what you would do if you knew you would not fail.

1. Say this out loud first then write down what you come up with. Don't think it through; when you write, let it flow from your heart. You don't actually have to do all the things you write down, it's just an exercise to get you to flow with ideas.

2. Look at your list and pick one idea that jumps out to you. Now write down a few of the characteristics and virtues of a person who has already developed and matured in that area. What gifts would they have? How would they interact with others? Examples: They would be compassionate; they would be creative; they would have confidence when they spoke to other people; they would know how to invest wisely.

3. Now that you have created a picture of who you are becoming, the next step is to close your eyes and

see yourself becoming the kind of person you just described. Ask God to make you this person. Really try to make the picture vivid and compelling.

If you find your mind telling you can't do it, then ask God to help you overcome it. For example, if your mind tells you, "I am too shy to ask the neighbors over," then ask God, "Help me overcome shyness."

You can go to www.personaldevelopmentgodsway.com to download the exercise so that you can do it on your computer.

Chapter 9

FINDING GOD'S WILL AND TIMING

GOD'S ULTIMATE PURPOSE FOR US IS LOVE

If you do not know, or you are not sure, what God's will is for your life, then you are not alone. People everywhere, young and old, are wondering what God is calling them to do. Most people are waiting for an audible voice from Heaven or a lightning bolt to strike them, but it usually does not happen that way. Quite often, God has been leaving us clues all of our life about what He wants us to do.

God's ultimate purpose for us all is to be in a loving relationship with Him. He wants first and foremost to be a father to us and love us unconditionally. The best way to know God's will is to know God's nature and His ways. Unfortunately, many Christians today do not have a healthy picture of God. Many see Him as a hard task-master waiting for us to mess up so He can smite us with trouble-some times. This is far from the truth. In most cases, it is satan who is bringing hard times, and God is getting the blame. God is full of grace, love, and patience. God is not as condemning as most people may think.

> *Therefore, there is now no condemnation for those who are in Christ Jesus, because through Christ Jesus the law of the Spirit of life set me free from the law of sin and death* (Romans 8:1-2).

After Jesus came to earth and died for sin, the old Law and rules were replaced with grace and forgiveness. After Jesus went back into Heaven, the Holy Spirit came into the world as the Comforter. The Holy Spirit can now reside in us and enable us to connect with God personally. The best way to get to know God is to spend time with Him. Read the Bible, pray, and do things to grow spiritually. The more we know His ways, the more likely we are going to recognize His will and purpose for us.

God wants to use each of us right where we are right now. You don't have to wait until later or until you are properly trained. If you are going to work each day to make a living and pay your bills and you do not feel fulfilled, then most likely you are lacking purpose. We all have a purpose to receive God's love and give it away to others. Once you grasp this purpose, then you can feel fulfilled every day of your life.

> *Whatever you do, work at it with all your heart, as working for the Lord, not for men, since you know that you will receive an inheritance from the Lord as a reward. It is the Lord Christ you are serving* (Colossians 3:23-24).

Your purpose at any given time is to love people and help them. There are so many opportunities at your place of work, school, or in your community to interact with people. Since many Christians have not realized this, there is a tendency to separate themselves from unbelieving co-workers, neighbors, or friends. They sit secluded, quietly reading their Bible at lunch or hanging out with other Christians.

God has called us to be a light to the world. We really need to interact with others. Be safe of course, but you can associate with non-Christians without sharing in their beliefs or sometimes crude conversations. Your job is not to lead everyone you meet to Jesus Christ. You can help them and interact with them and know that the kindness of God leads to repentance (see Romans 2:4). You can find out more about this concept in my book *Prophecy, Dreams, and Evangelism*.

HOW I DISCOVERED MY PURPOSE

In 1988, I was in my twenties and a new Christian. I wanted so much to find my calling and destiny. I remember sitting quietly, praying, and hearing a small voice inside that I knew was the Holy Spirit say, "Isaiah 61." Honestly, I don't think I had read the book of Isaiah at that point and had no idea what I would find. As I opened my Bible and read the first two verses, I fell on the floor crying.

> *The Spirit of the Sovereign Lord is on me, because the Lord has anointed me to preach good news to the poor. He has sent me to bind up the brokenhearted, to proclaim freedom for the captives and release from darkness for the prisoners, to proclaim the year of the Lord's favor and the day of vengeance of our God, to comfort all who mourn* (Isaiah 61:1-2).

I cried for the next six weeks every time I thought of these verses. Since I had just gotten off drugs and came out of the occult, it was comforting to think that God had a greater purpose and plan for my life. I went to my pastor and told him that I am supposed to preach!

Of course I had not been a Christian long enough and needed to study first. I was not able to go to Bible college at the time due to my financial situation, so I began reading and studying the Bible all the time. I went to Bible studies and conferences whenever I had the opportunity.

I prayed and asked God what to do next. Again, I felt God direct me to two sections of the Bible that explained how He wanted me to proceed. In Matthew 25:35-36, Jesus tells a parable about caring for people in need, praying for the sick in hospitals, and visiting people in prison. Then James 1:27 pointed out that true religion is caring for widows and orphans. I spent the next ten years diligently fulfilling these verses with every opportunity I would get. I ministered to people who were homeless or less fortunate, prayed for sick people, visited prison inmates, and helped widows and orphans, to name just a few.

These three simple verses built a foundation in my life that allowed me to get God's heart and perspective for people in need. You might say it was the best Bible college I could have ever attended. I preached my first sermon in 1991 at a homeless mission in San Francisco. This was just three years after God spoke to me about preaching the Good News to the poor.

In 1993, God spoke three more verses to me that became the foundation for my early evangelism training material. I used them as a guiding mission statement for the churches I started: Matthew 4:19; 22:37-40; and 28:19-20. Then in 2002, God gave me three more verses from the Book of Acts that became the basis for my message on Prophetic Evangelism and the thesis in my book *Prophecy, Dreams, and Evangelism*: Acts 1:8; 2:17-18; and 26:17-18. I highly recommend the entire Bible, but I got a lot of mileage over twenty years out of just a few verses that I practically applied to my life.

Finding and fulfilling God's plan for your life is usually easier than you think. Most often, it is as easy as loving God, loving other people, and helping others do the same thing.

FINDING YOUR CAREER

A lot of people I meet are in need of help with what type of career to pursue. Even if you are not pursuing a job or career, you can apply this section to other aspects of your life. Your career is anything you do with the majority of your time and life. This could be a stay-at-home parent, retiree, housewife, volunteer, or out in the workforce. God wants to use all of us where we are now!

The very first thing to do is to pray and ask God to speak to you about it. Begin to notice what you like to do and what brings you excitement. If you cannot answer the question of what you like to do, then you need to start by discovering your likes and dislikes. Try different jobs or volunteer at organizations.

Remember that your destiny can be like a "connect the dots" drawing. It will unfold over time. Years ago, people were encouraged to find a skill or trade and stick with it. The majority of people lived in the same house and retired from a job after 20 or more years. That is not the case today. There is a good chance that you will have several different careers and live in more than one city. Flexibility is the key in the new millennium.

There are many things that we could do in life, but we want to be sure that we commit them to God and they do not violate any of His principles in the Bible. In other words, if He calls you to do something, it will not be something illegal or harmful. God really does want us to succeed in all that we do. It takes time and trying different things to find your greater purpose.

Commit to the Lord whatever you do, and your plans will succeed (Proverbs 16:3).

So whether you eat or drink or whatever you do, do it all for the glory of God (1 Corinthians 10:31).

God is leaving us clues of guidance all the time. Some people call it coincidence or fate. I am convinced that God is trying to speak to us, but we have not been trained to listen. It is usually something so close to us that we may not recognize it.

In the book, *The Power of Who: You Already Know Who You Need to Know*, Bob Beaudine says that life provides clues. He encourages people to be like Sherlock Holmes and learn to detect the obvious. He mentions five clues to look for when you are pursuing your life purpose.

Clue 1: The Recurring Dream

Each of us has an assignment, a purpose, a dream all our own that we need to discover or rediscover. Maybe you've wanted to open a restaurant, become a fashion model, get your real estate license, or go back to law school. It's always been there and keeps resurfacing. Your dream is unique to you, and the fact that you still have the dream should speak loudly to you.[1]

Clue 2: Gifts and Talents

What are you just naturally good at? You've always been good at it. It comes easy to you. I'm amazed at how a real mechanic can open the hood of a car, poke around for two minutes, and pinpoint the problem. Sometimes he can just listen and know what's going on inside an engine. If you're mechanically minded, you know exactly what

I'm talking about, and that's a clue! If you're an artistic individual, however, you're probably not going to be fulfilled working in a garage. Talk to your "Who" (people who know you). They may have perspective of your gifts and talents that you're unable to see. What you're good at and what you enjoy are major clues to connecting with your destiny. Don't minimize their importance.[2]

Clue 3: Birds of a Feather

This is not complicated, so don't make it so. When you are on the right track, moving in the right direction, there will be a resonance with others moving along in the same stream. You're on parallel courses. There is an unspoken acceptance. You're all moving in the same direction. None of you are there yet; your final destinations may be different, but for now you're all on your way. Stay alert. If you have found your "stream," if you have been accepted by a "tribe"—don't take this for granted. It's another important clue.[3]

Clue 4: Rejection

Rejection is a severe teacher, and you'll most likely log some time in this classroom at some point in your life. But rejection can be even more instructive than favor because it forces you to come to grips with who you really are and who you're not. It lets you know where you don't belong and who you don't belong with. The sooner you get out of there and locate your right stream, the better off you're going to be. A lot of people try two or three streams, get rejected, and give up. Go where you're celebrated, not just tolerated.[4]

Clue 5: Do What You Love

Doing what you "love" is one of the most essential components of finding your dream. One of the great disconnects of life, a truly monumental error that people commonly make, is not allowing love to direct their course. Why? Because they don't know their own hearts, so they distrust themselves and their natural instincts. Just think of what would happen to the lion out on the plains if he didn't trust his own instincts. He would starve. When you allow yourself to be so programmed by the culture you're in that you become disconnected from your own heart, you're in major trouble. You render yourself unable to make decisions about what is best for your life and the lives of those you love. The real danger here is that you will begin to follow someone else's idea of success and fulfillment.[5]

Finding your clues can be as easy as listening to your heart, looking at what you love to do, asking others, and avoiding the things that cause large amounts of pain. Many are afraid to go after something that they love to do because they are afraid it may not be God's will for them. Let me be clear that not everything we desire is God's will. God is the giver of good gifts. He wants to give us our heart's desire. We just need our heart to be like His first. As we understand God's nature and our lives begin to reflect more of His character, then He can trust us, and we are more likely to feel the freedom to pursue our true dreams.

> *Delight yourself in the Lord and he will give you the desires of your heart. Commit your way to the Lord; trust in him and he will do this: He will make your righteousness shine like the dawn, the justice of your cause like the noonday sun* (Psalms 37:4-6).

KNOWING GOD'S TIMING

I mentioned previously that there are many teachings from the positive thinking and human development movements that indicate that you can do whatever it is you want. There is a difference between our own desires and God's desires for us. It could be that a job or something we want to do could get us sidetracked from something God wants.

When I started ministering in the homeless missions, I was offered a job to oversee a large inner-city housing project. It fit with all my experience working with the homeless, and I had the right skills. I was excited because I could take the leap from my corporate job to one with more ministry focus. I was so excited! I prayed for God's guidance and got advice from others. I determined that though it was a good job for me, it was not in God's timing.

I was disappointed, but looking back I can see that, had I taken it, I would have limited myself. God had different things in mind for me in the area of business that would later help finance my future ministry. I felt that God wanted me to stay in a business focus instead of full-time ministry at that time.

In 1994, just after turning down the inner-city housing job, I had also accomplished a major five-year career goal in my job as IS manager. I was feeling good about myself and giving thanks to God as I drove home that day. I asked God to speak to me about my next big career goal. I felt a nudge inside to turn on the radio, which was tuned to a Christian station. Immediately the speaker, Dr. Charles Stanley, said in his Georgia accent, "You listen here! Jesus is your goal." Wow, that was so powerful! I knew that God was still directing me to full-time ministry, even though I was still in business. So I took some steps to discover more about how to proceed.

After lots of prayer and advice, I left my corporate job and started a computer networking business. This allowed me to be a little more flexible with my time, so I could pursue ministry training and make a living at the same time. To be honest, it was not easy for me at the time. I wanted to be in full-time ministry, but I felt that God had a plan, so I stuck with it. Now I can see that I was already in full-time ministry as I went to businesses all over San Francisco and interacted with many people.

It was in my computer business that I learned the style of evangelism that I went on to teach people all over the world ten years later. I finally sold the business and went to start a church in a college town in the Midwest. Those were some of the most invigorating times of my life. It was so important to understand God's timing.

SIDETRACKS AND SETBACKS

As we pursue God's ultimate destiny for our lives, we will make mistakes. Sometimes we get sidetracked, and other times we have major setbacks and even get derailed. Sidetracks come from distractions of being too busy or unfocused. If you don't have a plan of what you want to do, it is very easy to get sidetracked. Clarity brings focus, and focus empowers our efforts because we become more intentional. Getting derailed from moving toward our destiny comes from anything that causes us to quit. This could be things like disempowering and ungodly beliefs about our self, poor decisions, fear, or even bad advice.

One thing to beware of is taking a job based on the amount of money it pays. Often, higher paying jobs came with a higher demand on your time and energy. You may want to seriously consider if you want to go down that road, especially if you have a family. Many couples take on high-stress, double income careers and then get used to living on higher pay, in a bigger house, with better cars. It is not a bad thing if you are wired for it and don't mind the extra headaches. Sometimes people want to just get back to the simple life again. It is not to say you cannot do it or that God is not calling you to, but be sure it truly is God leading you into a higher paying job. The novelty can wear off quickly, and making more money could result in having less peace and more problems in your life.

TRUST GOD TO GUIDE YOU

God really is the best counselor of all. Outside advice with people who believe in you helps too. You may want to avoid getting advice from people who don't believe in you. Never make a major decision based on one or two pieces of advice or just a vague feeling from God.

> *I will instruct you and teach you in the way you should go; I will counsel you and watch over you* (Psalms 32:8).

A mistake Christians make in trying to hear God for guidance in decisions is by using the "open door" strategy. Many people pray that God will close all other doors of opportunities except the one they should go through. This may work sometimes, but unfortunately, it does not always happen that way with God. He wants us to become mature in our decision making, so He will often give us choices to train us. It is like the way an earthly father helps his children. You can't make decisions for them all their life, or they never grow up. A better way to pray is that God will give you the wisdom to know which opportunity or door to take.

Christians most often use the "fleece technique" from Judges 6. Gideon asked God for a sign that He was with him. Gideon laid a fleece of wool on the ground and asked that the fleece would be wet and the ground dry. Sure enough, the next morning he found it wet and the ground dry. So he knew God had answered him. It is possible for God to answer these types of prayers. "God, if it is your desire for me to do this, then make this happen..." Again, God wants us to become mature in our decision making. Eventually God may not answer one of these prayers, and you will need to rely on other means of determining His will. I found that since the Holy Spirit is now in us, unlike in Gideon's day, we now can know God's will by the amount of peace we have. God's will always comes with His peace. Peace is the best fleece!

> *Peace is the best fleece!*

Jack Deere has some helpful advice regarding the use of fleeces:

> I have three cautions regarding this method of proving God's will. First, make sure the fleece is supernatural and cannot be manipulated by anyone concerned in the decision. Second, use fleeces sparingly and as a last resort. Excessive use of fleeces indicates a view of God that's more like a personal genie than a sovereign, almighty God. If we succumb to that view of God, it will lead to a loss of intimacy with Him. Third, remember that fleeces are a lower, less personal form of revelation. When we use a fleece, we are confessing either that God has not spoken to us, or that we could not hear Him with our hearts, or that what He did say to us has not given us the confidence to act.[6]

It will take practice to determine God's guidance. Never make a major decision on one or two vague feelings or dreams. If God is guiding you on something big, He will speak to you through a variety of different ways.

A friend of mine was praying about making a major move for his career. He contacted me because he had a dream that indicated that he should move to a specific area of the country, but he did not have a job lined up there. After discussing it further, we determined that it would be too risky to assume it was God guiding him based on one dream. A few weeks later, he called back and said that his wife had a similar dream and his prayer partner felt God was bringing a change to his life, but it was still too vague to take such a big step to relocate his family. Within a month he received a job offer in that area, and it was clear that he should move.

We need to wait on God's timing, especially if it involves your family and anything that has a high cost associated. Learning to hear God takes time, and you still need the input of others. It gets easier as you mature and get used to how God speaks. In the next chapter, I will cover in more detail how to hear the voice of God.

STAGES OF MATURITY

God sees you as whom you will become; however, you will still need to go through a process of development to get there. God is not impatient with immaturity. He actually enjoys relating to you as you grow. You would never expect a five-year-old child to drive a car. In the same way, God does not expect more from us than our current level of maturity allows.

As a pastor and a coach, I have found that most people are too hard on themselves when it comes to their growth and making mistakes.

You will grow faster once you can begin to see yourself as you are becoming and not who you are today. It increases your confidence and allows you to form the nature of Christ in you. As you grow and mature, God will test you for the purpose of promoting you into a greater level of maturity and influence.

Another way to accelerate and stay on track is to understand that we are all in different places in our journey. If we understand where we are in our maturity process, then we might not be too hard on ourselves when we mess up. We also need to know how to make a plan to get to the next level of life. When it comes to finding your life purpose and destiny, there are many factors to consider, such as God's timing and will or desire for you. The exercises in this book will help you to recognize the clues that God has been giving you all your life regarding your purpose and destiny.

Everyone goes through various stages of maturing. You can apply this to any area of your life: your career, emotions, finances, or whatever. For teaching purposes, I am applying it to spiritual growth.

Stage One: Building the Foundation

It is during this stage that you learn the basics needed for a healthy spiritual life, such as: prayer, study, worship, generosity, and gratefulness. This stage is all about discovery, renewing yourself, and building a foundation for your new-found life.

Stage Two: Personal Growth and Training

You begin to go deeper and develop more of God's character in your life. You start developing your spiritual gifts and the fruit of the Spirit. Your commitment to God becomes more of a personal relationship as opposed to obeying a set of rules. You also realize that there is a cost involved and that you are challenged to give up things that no longer serve you. You get practical training by taking classes at your church, conferences, and seminars. At this stage it seems like you can't get enough.

Stage Three: Maturing and Developing

You develop your specific ministry style and calling. You may get further training or even take Bible college courses. You have learned what it means to be a servant, and you would do anything that God asked you to do. At this point, your relationship switches to being more than just a servant; you now become a son or daughter, and God becomes your Father. You can be trusted with greater responsibilities and move from the need to continually be taught by others to others being taught by you.

Stage Four: Mastering Your Life

Ministry flows from you in everything that you do. Your focus is more on mentoring and developing others as opposed to your own ministry. You don't have to tell people what your gifts are because everyone knows based on your track record. You have greater authority and favor. You have come to a place where you know God's heart for any given situation. God trusts you because your desires are in line with His.

Many people are not aware that there are stages of maturity, so they get frustrated with where they are and either demand that others recognize them or stop pursuing growth. Most leaders stay at stage three, where the focus is on their ministry and fail to see that giving to others is an essential part of leading. Unfortunately, this is what is modeled for us in most churches. The ultimate place to be is mastering your life.

Striving and competitiveness are no longer a factor as you have embraced the mentality that the Kingdom of God is big enough for everyone to play a role. You give away more than you receive, but you understand the principle that "the more you give, the more you will receive," so you are fulfilled by giving to others.

I can easily recognize my journey through these steps, starting back when I first began to understand more about God's love. When I was building the foundation in my spiritual life, I was very fortunate to find some people at my church who taught me how to spend time with God and study the Bible. I learned how to journal, memorized some important Bible verses, and gained some experience with how to share my faith with others who were in need.

Within a few years, I got serious and stepped into the personal growth and training phase. I went to conferences, took classes, and practically applied what I learned by doing ministry at a convalescent home and a homeless mission in my area. As I matured and developed into a leader, I began getting specific training to help me learn to be a pastor and church planter. As I write this, I am just beginning to enter into the mastering life phase. I have a ministry, and I help lots of people. Something changed inside of me, where I want to see others succeed more than myself. It is a journey and a process.

God will test you along the way. He uses people, relationships, and situations to point out the things that are in you that are keeping you from advancing. Often, we will repeatedly experience the same types of setbacks or temptations. It is most likely that God is trying to point out something in your life that still needs work. Most people don't realize that nearly everything that happens to us is to test us or pinpoint growth areas. When we gain this perspective, we will be able to work hand in hand with God and not resist Him. It is up to you how long it will take you to advance to maturity. God loves you no matter what level you are at. It is not a contest or a pass or fail situation. It is an invitation to something more.

For many are invited, but few are chosen (Matthew 22:14).

The reason that few are chosen is that most people give up along the way. Quitting should not be part of your plan. You can restrategize, but don't give up!

> **Most people don't realize that nearly everything that happens to us is to test us or pinpoint growth areas. When we gain this perspective, we will then be able to work hand in hand with God and not resist Him.**

LIFE SEASONS

There are also life seasons, or periods of time that we all go through to bring us into spiritual maturity. Different than stages of maturity, life seasons are more situational. When you think of it, we don't really grow during times of blessing and success. As we look back on the more difficult times, we can see that it is in those times that we grew the most. These are similar to the seasons of the year, but they can happen at any time in your life or on the calendar. You don't have to go through them in any particular order.

Spring—A time of new growth. Change has happened recently, and things are being renewed.

Summer—A time of fun and blessing. It is like a mountain-top experience. We don't usually grow during these times, and we cannot live there, but summer times keep us going.

Autumn—This is a transition time when things begin to dry up and die. Old habits and behaviors start to fade away. It starts out looking pretty, but quickly changes. You are moving from one major season to another.

Winter—Everything is dormant, and the times are difficult. It is not easy to hear God or know the direction to go. This season is a test to strengthen our faith. This may also be known as a wilderness time.

Notice that many people in the Bible went through times of distress. Moses lived as a shepherd in the desert for 40 years. David had to hide so that Saul would not kill him. Jesus went into the wilderness to fast and pray for 40 days and was tempted by satan. It is good to recognize the season you are in. Usually wilderness times are to get you out of your own agenda and into God's desire for you. It is designed to change your focus to be more like God's.

You can shorten this wilderness time by recognizing the lesson that God wants you to learn and responding appropriately.

EXERCISE: WHAT ARE YOU DESTINED TO DO?

God has given us all a purpose to be in a personal relationship with Him and learn to love people. There are so many things we can do in life, and God gives freedom to choose what we want. Sometimes we will receive assignments to do for a season that will prepare us for the future. God has been leaving us clues all of our lives of what we are called to do. Let's uncover a few more clues.

1. What stage of maturity are you in right now? Describe why you believe you are in this stage.

2. What is your current life season?

3. Are there any dreams or things in your life that you have lost hope for or given up on?

4. Think about your favorite class, job, or any training or a degree you have received. What were the good things you liked about it? What do you dislike? What motivated you to pursue it?

5. What gets you excited or what do you enjoy and possibly have passion for? What is the thing that you perk up about when you talk with others?

6. Let's say for a moment you actually know what you are destined to do. Let it flow from within you. "I know I am destined to…" Write three to five things.

7. Find someone who knows you and talk to them about this exercise. Ask them if they have any insight about what you are good at and gifted to do.

You can go to www.personaldevelopmentgodsway.com to download the exercise so that you can do it on your computer.

ENDNOTES

1. Bob Beaudine, *The Power of Who* (Center Street, 2009), 85-86.

2. Ibid., 88.

3. Ibid., 88-89.

4. Ibid., 92-93.

5. Ibid., 93-94.

6. Jack Deere, *The Beginner's Guide to the Gift of Prophecy* (Ventura, CA: Gospel Light, 2001), 58.

Chapter 10

HEARING THE VOICE OF GOD

WE CAN ALL HEAR GOD!

Up until now I have been pretty practical with what I have shared with you. I realize that this section on hearing the voice of God may suddenly sound mystical and way out there for some people. Bear with me through this section, because it contains some very practical tips and key elements to help you find your destiny and to stay on track.

Learning to hear the voice of God is essential in discovering your destiny. After all, it is God's purposes that we want to fulfill, so hearing Him speak to us about it brings clarity. Wouldn't it make life easier if we knew His voice? Some Christians have stopped believing that God still speaks today. I am not going to convince you theologically or get into a debate, but I can tell you this: I have plenty of evidence in my own life to believe that God definitely still speaks to His people today.

Learning to hear the voice of God is a lifelong process, but it is simple enough that even a child can do it. Unfortunately, prophecy in general is very misunderstood today. It is not just a title given to someone who can hear God; though some people can process this calling to be a prophet. Prophecy needs to be viewed as a function in the life of a Christian and in churches.

The apostle Paul reveals that the purpose of hearing God is to know Him better and to discover more about what God has called you to do and to tap into His incomparably great power.

> *I keep asking that the God of our Lord Jesus Christ, the glorious Father, may give you the Spirit of wisdom and revelation, so that you may know him better. I pray also that the eyes of your heart may be enlightened in order that you may know the hope to which he has called you, the riches of his glorious inheritance in the saints, and his incomparably great power for us who believe* (Ephesians 1:17-19).

As we talk about hearing God, so many different things might go through your mind. Most people think that you have to be a prophet or have a prophetic gift to hear God. Some people are gifted by God to hear Him more clearly than others. I am convinced that we all can hear God, and that God wants us to hear Him.

Let's say you just thought of a friend that you have not heard from in years, and later that day you get a letter, e-mail, or phone call from them. The fact that you had that little intuition ahead of time was actually God speaking to you. How about when you're waiting in the checkout line at the supermarket? You get a feeling you should have gone to a different line; then you look over and sure enough, that line was moving much faster. That is God speaking to you. Let's say you are driving down the highway, and you get a distinct feeling inside that you should slow down. Then just ahead you see the police. Again, this is how God speaks to us.

Sometimes God speaks more clearly, but most of the time it comes in the form of a small, quiet voice inside us that, unless we train ourselves to listen to it, can be considered a coincidence. Everyone has experienced this sometime in their life. The way that spiritual gifts work is that some of us have the ability to hear more clearly from God than others. It does not make them more spiritual or that God likes them more than those who don't hear God quite as clearly. We all have different gifts, and we are all part of the Church that the Bible calls the Body of Christ. Each body is made up of different parts that have different functions.

> *Now you are the body of Christ, and each one of you is a part of it* (1 Corinthians 12:27).

Many Christians have thought that we should find the "gift" that God has given us. We may use one gift more than another, but we all have access to all the gifts through the Holy Spirit. This is most evident in the life of Jesus and His disciples. They all functioned in all different types of gifts, based on situations and people they encountered. So the fact is that you have access to the ability to hear God through the revelatory gifts mentioned in First Corinthians 12.

Hearing God does not need to be mystical. I like to think of the supernatural things of God as being a natural part of our lives. That would make us naturally supernatural. You do not have to be a prophet to hear the voice of God. As we develop this ability, it will help us to get into our destiny much more quickly if we are able to hear God guiding us. It is also beneficial to us in developing a deeper relationship with God.

PRACTICAL STEPS TO HEARING GOD

1. *Believe that God wants to speak to you.*

> *For God does speak—now one way, now another—though man may not perceive it* (Job 33:14).

Most Christians believe that God still speaks to people today, just not necessarily to them. And if we continually focus on not being able to do something, chances are we never will. But if we change our focus and accept that God loves us and longs to speak to us, there is a good chance we will begin to hear God in ways we never thought possible. There is a spiritual principle that unbelief chokes out supernatural experiences from God. An example of this is found in Matthew 13:58, when Jesus was not able to do many miracles due to the unbelief of the people.

God really does desire to communicate with us. Most of the time, we simply need to clear away some of the busyness in our lives to perceive what He is saying. He longs to convey messages of love, comfort, guidance, and warning through a variety of different methods. Maybe it is through dreams and visions (see Job 33:15-16), through the Bible (see Daniel 9:2), through a conversation we have with someone (wisdom), or through the arts (music, dance, paintings, sculpture). The possibilities are endless.

God longs for us to spend time with Him. Sometimes He gives us a puzzling dream just so we will search out the answer. And when we find the answer, it might seem insignificant, but God loves us so much that He is thrilled when we search for Him as we would for buried treasure. We can often miss God's still, gentle voice if we do not slow down enough to listen. I had a dream that a friend of mine was crying. The next day I sent an e-mail of encouragement and found out that he was going through a major "crisis" at work and my prayers really helped.

2. *Make sure you are at peace and have intentional times of quiet.*

> *But Jesus often withdrew to lonely places and prayed* (Luke 5:16).

We must have peace in our lives if we want to hear the voice of God. When we are hurried or stressed out, we are less likely to consistently hear Him. Many people hear God when they are in the shower or taking a bath. This may seem surprising, but it's because it's one of the few places where we are alone and able to listen.

It's good to set time aside regularly—daily, if possible—to quiet yourself. I mentioned previously that, for me, the best time is first thing in the morning. I know we are all wired differently, but morning seems to be a good time because the phone isn't ringing, there are fewer distractions, and things are the quietest. After a good night's sleep, we are more spiritually alert.

Each morning I try to spend a minimum of 15 minutes to get focused on God. I usually spend another 45 minutes or more praying, reading the Bible, and asking God to speak to me about my day. Maybe you don't have that kind of time, so do what you can. It would be nice if we all had quality time with God but the truth is, spending anytime with Him is beneficial. Part of my 45 minutes includes a prayer time while I am taking a walk. I use the exercise-prayer combination so that my body, soul, and spirit are all working together. I take a brisk walk, do stretches, or just get out and move around. When my life gets too hectic, I usually have ignored taking time to listen to God. Consequently, I end up getting less done than if I had spent time focusing on God first. When I spend time with God, He helps me to focus on what is important throughout my day so that I end up getting more done. I know, it's illogical, but as I talked about earlier, God is opposite.

There was a time in my life when no matter how much I had to do and how hard I worked, I always seemed to end the day feeling overwhelmed. So I did an experiment. For a week I spent two or three hours every morning walking, praying, reading the Bible, listening to an inspiring audio message, and prayerfully planning out my day. I discovered that I got more done and felt more fulfilled at the end of each day than if I had worked a grueling 12-hour day. I was even able to end my work just in time to have dinner with my family and did not have that nagging, overwhelmed feeling.

Since that time, I try my best to make it a priority to set aside time each day to hear God and get centered on Him. My whole day flows. I sometimes stray from this discipline but it does not take long to get back on track, especially after you experience the benefits. I tend to have fewer "fires to fight," and I get more accomplished.

If you are not taking time to get yourself centered or focused on God and hear Him each day, then I challenge you to make a plan right now to do just that. Fifteen minutes or less is all it takes. Start small, and slowly increase your time alone with God. I believe that you'll begin to want even more time with God once you get started!

I cannot overemphasize the importance of reading your Bible regularly. The more we know God's Word, the easier it will be to recognize His voice. We must know God's ways, His character, and His nature, which are found in the Bible. As we learn more of Who God is then we will be able to discern whether we are hearing from God, ourselves, or outside negative sources.

God will often speak to us by impressing a verse on our minds. Reading the Bible regularly will help condition us to be more spiritually sensitive. Sometimes God speaks to us clearly, and other times He is not as clear. God often conceals matters and requires those who really want more of Him to search for God as they would to uncover hidden treasure. If we spend time with Him, we will access the treasures of kings!

> *It is the glory of God to conceal a matter; to search out a matter is the glory of kings* (Proverbs 25:2).

3. Respond to what God says to you.

> *But the one who hears my words and does not put them into practice is like a man who built a house on the ground without a foundation* (Luke 6:49a).

As God begins to speak to you, it's a good idea to value these words and write them down. I realize that I am repeating points made previously about building a good foundation. This is because your destiny depends upon these fundamental daily practices. It is a good idea to get a notebook, a prayer journal, or type what you hear God saying in your computer—whatever fits your personality and style. Then get into the habit of writing down what you sense God telling you. This will help you keep track of them. Give thanks to God when you see them happening, because it helps your spirit to focus positively on God's good nature.

If we want to hear God consistently, we must be quick and faithful to respond every time He speaks. Sometimes God will remain silent until we do the last thing He told us to do. Stop for a minute and ask God to show you whether there is anything you need to respond to. God sometimes wakes me up in the middle of the night and speaks to me. Then I noticed this stopped happening, so I asked God to show me whether anything in my life was hindering my spiritual growth. Shortly after that I woke up at three o'clock in the morning and felt God nudge me to get up because He wanted to speak to me.

I dragged myself to the living room and waited. I didn't hear anything, so I turned on the television. On one of those middle-of-the-night infomercials, God spoke to me about how I handle my time and my need for more exercise. Once I applied what He revealed that night, my life changed radically. Later I realized He had already shown me this twice before in the past year. I had rejected it because it came in the form of an infomercial. Since I responded to this message, I again frequently hear God at night. Now I try to respond to God on a regular basis so that maybe He will not have to nudge me out of bed and I can get a better night's sleep!

4. Remove hindrances to hearing God.

> *Therefore, since we are surrounded by such a great cloud of witnesses, let us throw off everything that hinders...* (Hebrews 12:1).

On our journey to hear God, we will run into hindrances. A major hindrance to hearing God can be our own theology. If we were taught that God does not speak today, then this will affect our ability to hear Him. Our traditions or forms of worship can also be a hindrance to hearing God because they often limit when and how God can speak. I met someone recently who believed that we must pray in tongues before we can hear God. That is limiting because the gift of tongues is just one way of communicating with God.

When I first began to grow in my ability to hear God, I thought I had to be in a worship service to hear Him. I really don't know why, but I believed that if God was going to speak to me, it would probably be at church. The drawback to my way of thinking was that I was only in church once or twice a week, and the church I went to at the time had a quick, visitor-friendly type of service that did not allow much time to be quiet and listen to God. So I had to develop other ways to hear God. There is no one way or method for hearing God. He is multifaceted, and when we try to put Him in a box, we will miss the unlimited power and creativity available to us.

A third hindrance to hearing God is being too busy to listen. Sometimes we can fill our time with activities that appear worthwhile but actually hinder us from spending time hearing God. These activities can even take the form of Christian books, blogs, CDs, radio programs, or television. These are not necessarily bad for us, but if we substitute them for spending time with God, they can become hindrances. If this is the case for you, a solution might be to watch one less television program and instead watch and listen for God.

A fourth hindrance to hearing God is to assume we know what He is saying. This is called *presumption*. Often God speaks to us to reveal barriers and blocks in our relationship with Him. Our own ego and pride can block the real meaning of what God is trying to show us. We may think He is speaking about something or someone else and not about our own issues.

A man approached me with a dream that indicated that he was pursuing a destiny out of his own desires and strength and not out of God's calling on his life through the Holy Spirit. He assumed that the dream was not about him but was about someone else (he was the main character in the dream, and it was clearly about him). He rejected the wise advice that was given to him, and, as a result, he missed the opportunity to change his life and get back on track with what God wanted to accomplish.

HEARING GOD IN DAILY LIFE

Wouldn't it be great to hear God tell you to take a different way to work, and as you did, you avoided a huge accident on the freeway? Or to hear God subtly nudge you to buy flowers for your spouse, and when you got home you found that they had one of the worst days ever? How about hearing God tell you to go to the bank and remove a certain amount of money, and later that day you were in need of that exact amount of cash?

A while back, my wife was driving in the fast lane in fast moving bumper-to-bumper traffic in Los Angeles, and she heard the still small voice of God inside say, "Back off," so she did. Instantly, the car in front of her had a blow out, and had she not backed off she would have crashed. This is a dramatic example to illustrate that God wants to guide us every day in every way.

These are ways God wants to interact with us regularly; however, to hear God consistently and accurately takes practice.

> *But solid food is for the mature, who by constant use have trained themselves to distinguish good from evil* (Hebrews 5:14).

Many Christians are afraid of being deceived when it comes to hearing God. According to Hebrews 5:14, the remedy for this is to train yourself, which will take practice. One reason why many people do not hear God consistently is because they have not practiced listening. They may also have trouble discerning whether what they hear is from God, themselves, or other sources. Practice is required to grow and mature in our spiritual life.

People who work with money in the banking industry must be able to distinguish between real and counterfeit money. To be able to tell the difference between the two, you would need to become very familiar with real money to the point that you sensitized yourself to recognizing it right off the bat. Then, if you come across counterfeit money, you would immediately be able to recognize it just by touch or looks, because you have become sensitive through practice.

These same principles apply to hearing God. We must learn to be sensitive to the differences between God's voice, our own ideas, and those of demonic forces. The easiest way to do this is to study your own experiences. Let's say you hear God and there is clear evidence to confirm that what you heard was really God speaking to you. This might be something like an answered prayer or a situation that takes place for which you had no previous knowledge. Use a journal to record and study what it felt like to hear Him. Remember, how it came to you, the sense you had in your spirit, and the peace you had.

I was working as a computer consultant many years ago. One morning before work I was spending time with God and I sensed God tell me to wear a tie that day. I usually dressed business casual, but that day when I arrived at work, I was unexpectedly asked to meet my boss at the office of a client who was an affluent man in the entertainment industry. As I entered the client's office, I noticed my boss was also wearing a tie, and he was surprised to see me wearing one, too. I would have never done that without spending time to hear God each day.

So, how can we practice hearing God? First, ask God to begin to train you. Ask the Holy Spirit to make you sensitive to His voice. Write down what you feel God is speaking to you. Track your experiences and make notes on things you heard in advance that actually happened. We're not trying to predict anything; or be a prophet; we are simply asking God to speak to us so we can learn to hear Him better. I do various exercises regularly, and I teach students at my training seminars to do the same. Since this is just practice, you don't have to worry about getting it wrong.

DIFFERENT WAYS GOD SPEAKS TO US

There are so many different ways that God can speak to us. I have listed a few as a brief overview.

God Speaks Through the Bible

Sometimes God will speak through a verse in the Bible, and other times it is something that flashes through your mind. Not everything that we hear is necessarily from God. But practice will allow you to more easily discern what is and is not from God. When you hear from God, it will never violate His written word or ask you to do something illegal.

God Speaks Through Impressions or Pictures

Sometimes you may get something internally in the form of a picture in your mind or something quickly pops into your spirit. It may not necessarily be a complete thought but if you sense it's from God, be discerning, because not all our thoughts are from God. It could come as a single word or phrase, or a song. You may suddenly see a picture of a rose. If you were praying for someone else, you could say that God sees them like a rose. You then think about what it represents. A rose brings nice fragrance and beauty wherever it is.

There are also impressions from God that may come to you externally in the form of a vision or picture, or something externally that catches your eye. This could be repeated numbers on a clock, colors, or anything that God brings to your attention. For a split second you are drawn to the pen on the table, and God nudges you that writing is significant for you. Or you might remember that you wanted to write a thank-you note to a friend.

Remember that God usually speaks to us in a faint "still small voice" inside us. These are called impressions. Learn to trust that the Holy Spirit is speaking to you. We learn this by practicing, and we grow by experience. These impressions from God may vary in intensity. Let's use an example of a rating scale that measures the strength of the impression from one to ten; one on the scale are things that are vague and not clear; and ten being for things that are very clear and accurate. Any impression from God, regardless of the level, can help change your life.

Here's an example of how it works. I was with a friend, and we were talking to a woman who is not a Christian about her destiny. I had the impression that God really loved her. My impression was not all that remarkable, after all, doesn't God love everyone? But when I said it she got teary-eyed. Then my friend got an impression from God that there was someone in her life by the name of Susan, and she had a similar destiny as this person. She gasped as she shared with us that her sister had just passed away, and her name was Susan.

Now, I realize at that point we appeared to be psychics to the woman. We were able to let her know we were Christians and that God cares so much for her that He sent us to her to help. My impression may have been a level one on the scale, but it opened the woman to receive the level ten that my friend gave to her. It is not a contest, and one word or impression from God is not greater than another. The key is that it impacts us, encourages us, and changes us in some way, and ultimately it draws us closer to God, which is the main thing anyway.

God Speaks Through Dreams and Visions

Dreams at night can be a great way to hear God. Though not all dreams are from God, once you understand how God speaks through symbolic language, then you can trust God to guide you. Over one third of the Bible is made up of dreams and visions. Jesus often spoke in parables, and dreams are very similar to "night parables."

> *For God may speak in one way, or in another, Yet man does not perceive it. In a dream, in a vision of the night, When deep sleep falls upon men, While slumbering on their beds, Then He opens the ears of men, And seals their instruction. In order to turn man from his deed, And conceal pride from man* (Job 33:14-17 NKJV).

The great part about hearing God through dreams is that we don't always have to remember the dream or understand it to benefit from it. God will often give us direction for our lives through dreams and seal it away from our memory. Later, you may walk into a situation and have a feeling you have been there before. Some people call this déjà vu. I believe this happens because God gave us direction in a dream that we could not remember, and when we are living it out later we get that strange feeling that we have experienced it before. So sometimes the best dream we can have is when we know we have dreamed but we cannot remember the details. Let me explain what I mean.

We can receive instructions and guidance through dreams that are essential for our purpose and our destiny. The more clearly or directly God speaks to us, the greater our responsibility to respond to what He tells us. By concealing His instructions in a dream, God can bypass our natural mind and even keep us from being prideful and from doing things in our own strength instead of His. Sometimes God has to wait until we are unconscious (sleeping) to speak to us so we will not argue or be fearful of what He wants us to do.

Another example of how God can use a dream is when you actually remember the dream, but He seals away the meaning of it. We can have a dream from God that seems very significant, but we do not understand the interpretation or how it applies to our life. This happened in the life of Joseph in the Old Testament.

In Genesis 37, Joseph received two powerful dreams about his destiny. The dreams indicated that his brothers and his parents would one day all bow down and serve Joseph. Even his father, Jacob, did not understand the meaning of this dream. The result was that Joseph's brothers became jealous, so they sold him to some traders, and Joseph ended up a slave in Egypt. Later, in Genesis 41, God turned Joseph's mishaps into a huge blessing that helped save the entire world from a famine. His dreams came true years later. A lesson we might learn is to be careful who we share our dreams with! And, that our dreams may take years to come to pass, so be sure to track and review them.

How does this relate to your destiny? Maybe you have wondered how your life ended up the way it is. Often, like Joseph, we end up far from where we started, and it may seem that the promises and dreams that God gave us will not come to pass. Just this year, I turned 50 years old, and as I write this book, I am seeing dreams and things that God spoke to me over 20 years ago about my destiny beginning to unfold. Had God revealed all the details ahead of time, I probably would have tried to make things happen too soon. God is faithful, and we can trust Him as a loving father. Hold on to your dreams and be open to the element of God surprising you with good things from Heaven.

Other Ways that God Speaks to Us

There are many ways that God can speak to us, but I don't have the time in this book to go into all the details. Jesus said over 15 times that we must have "eyes that see and ears that hear." He was referring to seeing and hearing spiritually. Jesus taught powerful principles about the Kingdom of God by using parables. These symbolic stories from real-life situations conveyed a deeper spiritual truth. Even His disciples who were close to Him did not understand this way of communication at first. You can learn a lot about God's hidden language by studying Jesus' parables and how He described their meanings to the disciples.

God may speak to us through other people. What may seem like a normal conversation with a friend could be God trying to communicate something to you. God can speak through movies, music, and the arts. I was traveling on a plane, and the movie *Spiderman* was playing.

Through this movie, I was able to see the modern parable that God was speaking to us today. If we Christians stop using our spiritual gifts and supernatural abilities like Peter Parker did, then crime or evil in the world will increase over all. His neighbor, Mary Jane, is symbolic of the Church. Peter Parker loved her, but she was in love with an evil boy who represents the world in my comparison. I could go on and on. I was encouraged when I saw this movie to continue moving forward even when times get tough and I am rejected by people around me.

God can speak through nature or natural things. Take a walk in the woods and allow creation to speak to you through its beauty and splendor. Often things that happen in the natural realm are reflective of what is happening in the supernatural. Recently there was a conference in which a group prayed for revival and a new move of God. The same weekend a new oil field was discovered there, and it was the biggest in that area's history. This is symbolic of God bringing something new in the spirit to that town.

There are other ways to hear God which may include things like supernatural experiences, angels, and hearing an audible voice from Heaven. These are all very biblical, and though they are not as common, they cannot be ruled out as a means to hearing God.

DESTINY DREAMS

Some dreams pertain to your destiny. After interpreting thousands of dreams for people, I began to notice a common pattern. Some dreams indicate that there is something more for people to fulfill in their lives. We won't go into the entire teaching about understanding dreams, but I have highlighted a few dreams that you can watch for and how to respond.

Any reoccurring dream is an indicator that God wants to either do something new in your life or is drawing your attention to change something. Once you either establish the new behavior or take care of the issues, then these reoccurring dreams will stop.

Science has proven that everyone dreams. If you cannot remember your dreams, it may be due to several different reasons. It is possible that you need more peace in your life, or, it can just be how you are wired—some people just don't remember their dreams. Another possibility is that God is concealing your dreams similar to the passage in Job 33:14-17.

Flying without an airplane: These dreams indicate higher destinies to fulfill. You have creativity and the ability to rise above situations and have great flexibility.

Running/being chased: Usually it seems like something evil is trying to get you. If this is the case, then satan wants to stop you from something good. The positive part of this is that you have a destiny to help a lot of people; why else would something try to stop you? The key is to not be afraid and begin to ask God to show you what it is you are destined to do.

Showing up late: This dream is showing you that there is something that you are called or destined to do, but you are currently lagging in the process of accomplishing it. It is a heads-up to be more diligent in your pursuit.

Being naked: Showing up in a dream with no clothes on when everyone else in your dream is dressed is common and actually positive. It shows that you are a person who is open and vulnerable with others. This is an indicator in the type of vocation or gifting you have. Most likely people feel safe around you and will tell you their problems, so you have the ability to help people through counsel or advice.

Taking a test: We are always being tested by God for the purposes of promotion and advancement. An indicator that you are being tested is a dream where you are taking a test. If you feel like you are not prepared, then it indicates the need to get more training or help.

Being in school: These dreams indicate that you are in a time of learning new things. This is valuable time in developing yourself for your life purpose.

Having a baby or being pregnant: Babies are symbolic of new life. They are usually not literal but instead symbolic of something new coming. A new job, ministry, gift, idea, invention, or something creative is coming to you. If you are given or find a baby in a dream, then it is something someone else was called to do but did not do it, and it is being given to you to accomplish. If the baby is big for its age or has hair and teeth early, it means you will mature in your new gift quite quickly.

Teeth coming loose or falling out: This indicates the need to get wisdom or advice about your situation.

Negative dreams or nightmares: When we have nightmares or anything negative, it is not usually God's will for our life. These types of dreams are showing us that something wants to stop us or hold us back from all the good things that God has for us. Since these types of dream show satan's will and not God's will, then we need to flip them around and begin to pray the opposite will happen. The only true reality for you is God's intentions.

STEPS TO UNDERSTANDING DREAMS:

1.   Write your dreams down and save them.

2.   Pray for divine understanding.

3.   Make notes and do research.

4.   Follow through on direction you receive.

5.   Study the Bible, especially the dreams and parables.

6.   Learn to think metaphorically or symbolically.

Dreams are very subjective, so symbols may change from dream to dream. The context of the dream is what is important. Is it about your work, family, ministry, life? The symbols are important, so look first in the Bible to understand a symbol. If you cannot find it, think of the symbol like a parable. What does the symbolized thing do, or what relationship does it have to you, in your waking life? For example, a pickup truck is used most as a work vehicle or to carry things, whereas a school bus carries a number of people to a place of learning. An alligator has a big mouth, so it might represent gossip. When trying to understand dreams, be careful of using a dream symbols book. Many of the popular dream symbols books are inaccurate and are based on psychology, as opposed to biblical symbolism.

Dreams are not always easy to understand, but like anything else, the more we value and study them, the more we can recognize when God speaks to us. Since we spend about a third of our life sleeping, it is a great way to gain more insight into our destiny with a minimal amount of effort. I have additional training resources on understanding dreams on my Web site.

EXERCISE: HEARING GOD

Learning to hear the voice of God is a lifelong process. Sometimes we can hear Him clearer, and other times it is almost as if He is silent. If you used to hear God but don't anymore, then think back to one of the last times you heard Him. Is there something He asked you to do, but you haven't done it yet? This could be the block.

Here are a few exercises to hear God more clearly. Don't be discouraged if you are not able to hear Him clearly on any or all of these. It is a process.

1. Hearing God through the Bible: Ask God to give you a verse in the Bible. Close your eyes and don't think hard; just wait until something comes into your mind. This may take a few tries to get something practical. Try it every day for five days or until you receive something that you have peace about. Write down your experiences in a journal, then pray the verse back to God and ask Him to fulfill it in your life. Try to share things with the person that is positive and uplifting. Remember, God is positive and it will help to encourage someone.

2. Hearing God through writing: Take a piece of paper or use your computer, and begin to write what you feel God is speaking to you. Think of it as a love letter from your father. Let it flow from deep inside you. Again, it should be positive and uplifting and will not condemn you. God loves you and wants you to succeed.

3. Hearing God through an object: Pick up an object that is near you right now. Hold it in your hand and ask God to speak to you about yourself based on this object. Look at all sides of the object, read it, and think symbolically. Write down what He tells you.

4. After practicing the first three exercises, ask God to speak to you about your purpose and destiny. Write down what you sense God is saying to you.

5. Have you had any of the "destiny dreams" mentioned in this chapter? Are you currently having a reoccurring dream? What can you learn about your life based on the dreams you are having?

6. Now ask God to speak to you about your destiny. Each day for the next few days, ask God to speak to you about your destiny. Record anything you hear in your journal.

You can go to www.personaldevelopmentgodsway.com to download the exercise so that you can do it on your computer.

Chapter 11

THE POWER OF CONNECTIONS

Did you know that everything you hear, speak, think, eat, and virtually everything you do has some type of connection with all the other areas of your life? So when one aspect of your being is out of balance, it can affect your entire being. I call it the power of connections because our thoughts, words, and actions all affect one another. We tend to compartmentalize our lives—we have our personal life, spiritual life, career, or work life—but in reality they are all essential parts of our one life.

THE CONNECTION OF MOVEMENT AND LANGUAGE

When I say the word *communication,* most people think of the spoken language. Though language plays a role in communication, not all communication is verbal. Studies show that body language accounts for 97 percent of our communication and only 3 percent through spoken words. Have you noticed that you are always assessing a person based on the way they stand, look at you, or even shake your hand? Your mind begins to make assumptions about someone before they even speak.

Most people don't realize the connection of movement and language in our lives. The way you speak and move your body has a direct correlation to how you feel about yourself and how others feel about you. As a public speaker, if I stood hunched over in front of people, talking very slowly and quietly about getting excited about your destiny, what would you think? "This guy is not too impressive." The way we speak and move is very important in connecting with others.

LANGUAGE

Our language consists of two parts, and both are important— inner dialog and outward dialog.

Inner dialog is what you say to yourself when you're thinking. It is the voice in your head. As I mentioned previously, it is a good idea to be sure that you are being positive and affirming to yourself.

Outward dialog is the way you speak to other people. You can tell a lot about a person by the words they use when they speak. Notice if they are generally positive or negative, encouraging or discouraging, doubtful or hopeful, fearful or confident. Your language toward others displays how you truly feel. Are you being loving and supportive or sarcastic and cutting?

People tend to give one another clues about how they feel, what they value, or what they need through the way they talk, their body language, and facial expressions. But most people are not aware of it because they are not trained to perceive it and they listen with their ears only. Our goal in life is to be an encourager of other people by listening with our heart and the help of the Holy Spirit.

CONNECTION OF LISTENING

Most people don't like to listen to others, yet they value being listened to. The ability to listen is really an art that, through practice, increases your ability to focus on what a person is really saying.

Quite often, people came to Jesus and asked a question. His answer spoke to their hidden need or revealed their hidden motive. To pinpoint this, Jesus often asked them a question back. Too often we launch into our own story, advice, or latest teaching without regard to the needs of the person approaching us.

THREE LEVELS OF LISTENING

- Listening from your feet

- Listening from your head

- Listening from your heart

When you listen from your feet, the lowest form of listening, you are not interested at all in what the person has to say. You are more ready to walk away than to help the person. You have no real concern about the person or their situation. It is apparent when someone is not listening to us. They are distracted by things around them: maybe they take a phone call or change the subject over to their own needs.

When you listen from your head, you are attempting to logically solve the person's problems. Most people simply want you to listen to them, and feel that you care. They are not usually talking to you to get your opinions on their problems.

The most effective and highest level of listening is from your heart. We need to have compassion for the person who is speaking. Not to try to fix them or fill them up with advice or stories, but to walk with them even for a brief moment and feel what they feel. Letting someone know you care involves giving them good eye contact. Don't be distracted by looking around or taking a cell phone call. Listening from the heart causes the person to feel loved and cared for. The way you listen to others tells you a lot about yourself. If you are not listening to others, then most likely people are not listening to you.

CONNECTION OF THE BODY, SOUL, AND SPIRIT

God created us as body, soul, and spirit integrated into one person. An easy way to understand this is that it is similar to God being three parts: God the Father, the Son, and the Holy Spirit—yet all three are still one God. We are made in His image. If you were raised in the modern Western world, you probably view these aspects of your life as separate from each other.

As Westerners, we tend to see our spiritual life separately from our work or career life. The same goes with our physical body, our emotional life, and so on. This is a disadvantage because we miss the fact that we are made up of a body *and* a soul *and* a spirit—and if one part of our being is suffering—our entire being suffers.

The holistic biblical view of a person is that we have three main parts that are all integrated into one:

- Body—consists of our flesh, blood, and bones, or the physical part of our lives

- Soul—our mind, thoughts, emotions, and desires

- Spirit—our divine connection to God; it allows us to have a relationship with God, gives us wisdom from God, and the consciousness of what is right and wrong.

May God himself, the God of peace, sanctify you through and through. May your whole spirit, soul and body be kept blameless at the coming of our Lord Jesus Christ (1 Thessalonians 5:23).

CONNECTION OF THE BODY, SOUL, AND SPIRIT

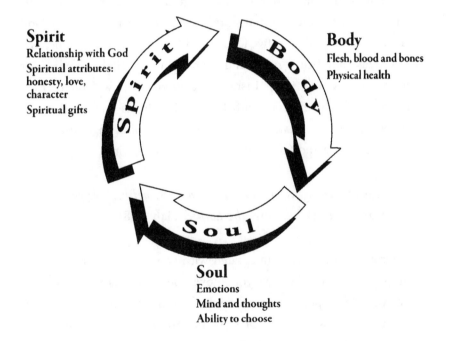

Spirit
Relationship with God
Spiritual attributes:
honesty, love,
character
Spiritual gifts

Body
Flesh, blood and bones
Physical health

Soul
Emotions
Mind and thoughts
Ability to choose

If your body is sick, it will affect your entire well-being. If your soul is sick, emotionally then it will affect both your body and your spiritual life. If your spirit is sick, (in other words, if you are not maturing in your connection with God), then you will rely more on your soul or thoughts to guide you. God created us to be guided by the Spirit—not our souls or bodies.

If we allow our body—the desires of our flesh—to govern or guide us, we get out of balance leading to various kinds of excesses to satisfy physical sensations like hunger, sleep, sex, etc. When the body rules, there is an overemphasis on physical comfort and satisfaction. If we are guided by our soul—our thoughts, emotions, or perceptions—we'll experience a limited understanding of God and the Christian life. For instance, God does not always seem to us to be "logical," and the Christian life should have room for the supernatural aspect of God. This includes miracles, spiritual gifts, dreams, and visions.

We were ultimately created to be guided by God through the Spirit. Our mind and emotions are necessary and part of how God created us. Our goal is to live a balanced life in which we are healthy in all areas, not being ruled and guided by our flesh, intellect, or emotions (body and soul). Instead, we need to allow God to flow through our body and soul with His Spirit. This is a major shift for most people because many of us were raised to think that all of these areas are separate and God only deals with our Spirit.

"For my thoughts are not your thoughts, neither are your ways my ways," declares the Lord (Isaiah 55:8).

Because your body is integrated with your soul and spirit—then your physiology or the way you move your body can dramatically affect your life—positive or negative. Consider the process that you may go through when you worship God. You may begin by singing a song; you clap or raise your hands; you begin to picture in your mind images of God sitting on the Throne and all the angels worshiping. As you do this your spirit begins to connect with God, and for brief moments you feel a divine connection with Heaven. Notice that you started out using your voice and moving your body, then your mind joined in (all are soul), and then your spirit begins to respond by connecting with God on a deeper level.

Have you ever been in a group of people as you pray for a particular person? You stretch out your hand; you begin to speak or silently ask God to touch them. You visualize God touching the person. As you do this, your spirit responds in faith, and you may feel a sense of peace or God's presence. Again, you start out using your body, then your soul, and your spirit respond in the process. God created all three areas, and we use them all to interact with the divine.

CONNECTION OF YOUR PHYSICAL BODY

I want you to take just a moment to do an experiment. Think of a time in your life when you were very sad or down or depressed. Something happened that upset you.

Now do your best to imitate how you felt, feel the feelings, connect with the memory of how you felt when you were down or depressed. Seriously, do your best to get depressed for a minute.

Put your body in the same position you may have had then. Now notice your body. Are your shoulders back or forward? Is your breathing deep or shallow? Is your head up or down? Are you sitting or standing upright and tall, or are you slumped? Is your future bright or dark?

OK, shake it off and come back to reality.

Now think of a time in your life when you were excited. You just won a contest, your bowling team came in first place, you got a new puppy, you got a promotion at work...whatever. Think about a time in your life when you were excited and relive that experience for just a moment. Feel how you felt then. Position your body or stand the way you stood.

Now notice your body. Are your shoulders back or forward? Is your breathing deep or shallow? Is your head up or down? Are you sitting or standing upright and tall or are you slumped? Is your future bright or dark?

> *You can change the way you feel by changing the way you move.*

Nearly everyone doing this exercise will experience the same results: When you are depressed or down your shoulders are usually forward, your breathing is shallow, your head is down, you are slumped, and your future is dark. When you are excited, everything is the opposite. Your shoulders are back, your breathing is deep, your head is up, you are standing tall, and your future is bright.

There is a direct connection between the way you move and position your body and the way you feel. It is like a recipe. You mix specific things together, and you will get a result. You may have already known that your body responds to your emotions. But it is also true that your emotions will respond to your body.

Try this exercise. Physically position yourself the way you did when you felt excited. Look up and tilt your head back. Stand strong with your feet apart and put a big smile on your face. Now smile up to God and keep smiling.

Once you are feeling excited and confident, don't change anything with your body—keep looking up—keep smiling and try to feel depressed *without* changing anything about your body position. You can't do it! When you are smiling and laughing, you can't feel depressing feelings! So if you want to change the way you feel, the way you make decisions, the way you think, you can start by changing the way you move and breathe.

People think I am joking, but I am very serious. I do this all the time. If I start to feel down or doubtful, I jump to my feet, put some happy music on, and within a few minutes I have changed my outlook on life.

In the Bible, when David was down he strengthened himself in God and got a new outlook on his situation.

> *Now David was greatly distressed, for the people spoke of stoning him, because the soul of all the people was grieved, every man for his sons and his daughters. But David strengthened himself in the Lord his God* (1 Samuel 30:6 NKJV).

You can change the way you feel by the way you move your body. Make a habit of walking with your shoulders back and breathing more deeply; be strengthened in God (spirit), and your mind and your emotions will begin to have more of a positive response. You will begin to feel better and become more confident. This change will ultimately affect your entire being, including your spiritual life.

Most people don't breathe deeply enough. When you take a deep breath, be sure to allow your stomach to rise instead of your chest. This will allow oxygen into the lower area of your lungs and will go directly to the area of your brain that stimulates creativity.

Remember to take at least five deep breaths a couple of times a day or when you are feeling stressed.

CONNECTION OF SPIRIT WITH YOUR EXPERIENCES

Many Christians have been taught that you should not place much value on feelings. The result is that there are people walking around doing their best to be spiritual and ignoring their feelings.

Though we should not allow our emotions to overpower or control us, God created this part of us as well. There is an element of truth in this type of thinking—because we should *not* be guided strictly by our feelings. We should be guided by the Spirit of God. But our feelings are a good barometer to tell us when things are not going well. So it is okay for us to *feel* our feelings.

This misunderstanding of not trusting your feelings is based loosely on Second Corinthians 5:7, where Paul says that *"We live by faith, not by sight."* If we are guided by the Spirit, then our feelings will no longer control us—but they still play a key role in our spiritual experience. Our feelings and our experiences in life play a role in helping us get to our destiny. Here is a key verse that reveals this principle:

> *For the kingdom of God is not a matter of eating and drinking, but of righteousness, peace and joy in the Holy Spirit* (Romans 14:17).

This is saying that we all have a connection with God's Kingdom or our spiritual life—but it is not just through the rules about what we eat. Paul was referring to religious practices of his day that were ritualistic. Paul was addressing the fact that in his day some Christians believed you could not eat certain foods and still be a Christian. He explains our connection with God: It involves righteousness, peace, and joy, which all come through God's Spirit.

Take a closer look, and you'll see that all three aspects of the Kingdom of God relate to the three aspects of your life: spirit, body, and soul:

- Righteousness cannot be obtained on your own. It comes only from God's grace. This is God's connection to your spirit.

- Peace is a feeling or experience. How do you know you have peace? You feel it in your body. This is God's connection to your body.

- Joy is an emotion—how do you know you have joy? You feel or experience it. This is God's connection to your soul.

Notice that two out of three aspects of God's Kingdom involve an experience or feeling. Two-thirds of our connection with God involves experience, so ignoring your feelings may not be a good idea. You can use your feelings to show you areas of your life that need work. Or you can turn around negative feelings to be positive.

HEALING OF EMOTIONS

Since we are integrated, then things like emotional wounds can affect all the other areas of our life. Things that happened to us in the past can cause us to overreact in the present. Some people refer to this as getting your buttons pushed. This is where a present situation triggers something within you usually from your past, even if the person didn't mean it to be hurtful. You then begin to respond based on a past experience or hurt, usually having nothing to do with the current situation. An emotional hurt will also cause you to respond at a much higher level of intensity than the situation warrants.

Maybe someone does something that you don't like and you respond at an anger level of 9 on a scale of 1 to 10, when it may have been more appropriate to respond at a 3 or 4. Healing emotional hurts does not have to be a painful process. You don't have to relive all the traumatic experiences or spend hours recounting all that happened to you. Whether you have any of these issues or not, please consider the following to understand how to help others as well as yourself.

HOW JESUS DEALT WITH THE EMOTIONAL HURTS OF OTHERS

I myself have walked through the process of inner-healing. I suffered from an extreme level of emotional and sexual abuse when I was young. For years I went to therapy. I cried and cried at church altars. The pain inside me was so terribly bad. It actually felt like a knife in my heart. I had prayer counseling and deliverance prayer; I tried nearly everything, but I still ached inside.

The prayer and counseling worked to a small degree. I would see small amounts of healing, but when things got difficult, I often reverted to old ways of dealing with pain by overworking or shutting down emotionally to numb the pain. It helped short term, but in the long run, the same feelings and issues kept coming up over and over.

During this process I found that many of the popular therapy methods, though they were good and worked to some degree, too often took years if not decades to bring freedom to a person. Don't get me wrong, I think we need therapists and counselors. My wife is a marriage and family therapist, and she agrees with me that we also need to look to the miraculous power of God along with counseling. She noticed that if she combined prayer and the power of God along with counseling, she saw a dramatic increase in a person's ability to recover.

MY BREAKTHROUGH WITH PERSONAL HEALING

It was 1992, and I was getting lots of deep healing in my life. I was reading the Bible and noticed that after Jesus was crucified and was buried, Mary Magdalene went to his tomb on Sunday morning. The stone in front of the tomb was rolled aside. She knelt down and looked inside, but His body was not there. He had been resurrected from the dead, but she didn't know where he was. She was crying because of her great loss.

> *Then the disciples went back to their homes, but Mary stood outside the tomb crying. As she wept, she bent over to look into the tomb and saw two angels in white, seated where Jesus' body had been, one at the head and the other at the foot. They asked her, "Woman, why are you crying?" "They have taken my Lord away," she said, "and I don't know where they have put him." At this, she turned around and saw Jesus standing there, but she did not realize that it was Jesus. "Woman," he said, "why are you crying? Who is it you are looking for?" Thinking he was the gardener, she said, "Sir, if you have carried him away, tell me where you have put him, and I will get him." Jesus said to her, "Mary." She turned toward him and cried out in Aramaic, "Rabboni!" (which means Teacher)* (John 20:10-16).

As I read this, my eyes were opened to a key to getting over painful events from the past. Mary was traumatized by witnessing the brutal beating and death of her friend, teacher, and Lord.

Her pain was due to the loss of someone dear, who may have been the first to ever care for her.

NOTICE THESE KEY ELEMENTS

The Tomb: The other disciples had spent time mourning at the tomb of Jesus and then went back home, but Mary stayed there crying. Mary looked into the tomb and was focused on her loss. This is similar to when we focus on the loss and pain of our past. Too often, we can stay continually focused on the tomb of our past. There is no life in the tomb. Don't get me wrong, it is important to take time to deal with grief and loss, and yet there comes a time to look in a new direction. You cannot live your life in front of the tomb of your past perpetually. Get help to get through it.

Where was Jesus? He was behind her. Mary had to stand up and turn 180 degree from the tomb. This symbolizes the need for us to turn our focus away from our past, and from our pain and loss. There is a time to grieve, but if you keep your focus on your loss, you will not recover from it.

Then there was the Gardener. Jesus came disguised as someone who helps cultivate new life. This symbolizes that when you turn your focus away from your loss, God is there to help things grow and bring life.

Meanwhile, back at the tomb, Mary saw two angels who were able to give her direction. They represent that inside every painful experience there is a blessing from God, if we can only recognize it.

After reading this, I started to recognize that in every painful experience there was a gift. By simply changing your focus, you can allow the past to strengthen you and give you the necessary tools to help others who are camped out at their tombs.

When Jesus said, "Mary," her eyes were opened, and she immediately recognized him. Often, we are not able to recognize the work of God in our painful situation. God will do something to let us know that He knows our personal situation. In Mary's case, He spoke her name, and she then recognized Jesus in her midst. As you get in a close relationship with Him, God will find ways to let you know He loves and cares for you specifically. He will speak to you in some way that will let you know He knows you.

A key to a brighter future is the power of refocusing away from the past. If you get a new perspective, then painful times can help strengthen you to fulfill your destiny in ways you can never imagine.

THE CROSS AND THE RESURRECTION

Here's another discovery I made. I have the opportunity to travel and minister in churches all around the world. I have observed very often only part of the message of transformation is being taught. I don't think this is intentional; it is because most people are not aware of this. Each week thousands of invitations are made to come to the altar as preachers plead, "If you are hurting, then come to the foot of the cross." This is a very true and powerful statement, and, yes, we need to go there with our pain.

However, there is an additional teaching that is being left out, and it is the key to people not coming back to the altar week after week. We take our hurts to the Cross because of what Jesus did there... He died for our sin, sickness, and disease. So, yes indeed, bring all your pain, your sickness, and shortcomings to the foot of the Cross of Christ. But don't stop there because after the cross of Christ came the Resurrection. Too often people go to the Cross for prayer and are not instructed to leave their hurt and pain there and walk away free from it because of the resurrection power of Christ.

The Cross of Christ is the first step to healing our old life, but the Resurrection is the overcoming power needed to live a new life:

Jesus said to her, "I am the resurrection and the life. He who believes in me will live, even though he dies" (John 11:25).

And if the Spirit of him who raised Jesus from the dead is living in you, he who raised Christ from the dead will also give life to your mortal bodies through his Spirit, who lives in you (Romans 8:11).

You can't change the past, but you can change how the past affects your present and your future. The power of God is available to completely transform your life.

> **You cannot change the past, but you can change how the past affects your future.**

FORGIVENESS

I read an article called, "Forgiveness: A Key to Better Health." The following quotation says it all:

> Don't just talk about forgiveness. Researchers are finding that really forgiving others has important effects on your health. Forgiveness has long laid the foundation for spiritual well-being in the Judeo-Christian tradition. But scientific research now suggests its healing power may extend beyond the sacred realm. Research shows links between forgiveness and physical and mental health.
>
> While this may come as some surprise to secular scientists, psychologist Dan Shoultz says, "God has created the need to give and receive as an important part of our makeup as human beings. We were designed by God to not hold onto anger, revenge, bitterness, and resentment," Shoultz says. "When we do, it is destructive to our being, leading to a slow and insidious breakdown of the entire system."[1]

Many people suffering from stress, anxiety, bitterness, and depression may very well need to forgive themselves and others. The effects of unforgiveness are not only physical but spiritual. The Bible links forgiving others with being forgiven by God:

For if you forgive men when they sin against you, your heavenly Father will also forgive you (Matthew 6:14).

Be kind and compassionate to one another, forgiving each other, just as in Christ God forgave you (Ephesians 4:32).

If you have unforgiveness you may find yourself:

- Thinking about getting revenge

- Wanting something bad to happen to a person

- Holding a grudge

- Talking about someone behind their back

- Obsessing with a memory of something someone did to you

Forgiving a person does not mean that you agree with what they did. You can forgive a person, but trust may need to be rebuilt for the relationship to be restored. You can also forgive a person who is no longer living. You can forgive someone without telling them that you forgave them. It is the act of forgiveness that frees things up in the spiritual realm. Forgiving yourself is necessary as well. Just as unforgiveness can create negative effects—forgiving creates a positive atmosphere.

STEPS TO FORGIVENESS

- List out the offenses that people have done that continue to bother you. You may have already forgiven them, but if you are still feeling the ill effects, then repeat the exercise.

- Go through them one by one and ask God to give you the strength to forgive them. Say, "In the name of Jesus, I forgive _____ for _____."

- Visually see yourself releasing the person. See the hurt you have been carrying vanish into God's light or the Cross of Christ.

- If you need to, write a letter to the person or to God. You don't have to mail it. This can be to a person no longer living or someone still alive.

- Be honest and feel the effects this pain has had on you, not the pain itself. The goal is to let it be released from you so it no longer affects you.

- Decide if you want to talk with the person or not, but realize that confrontation may bring up the same response as you had before. Only do this if it is safe. It is not necessary to talk to a person to forgive them.

- Realize that forgiveness and healing is a process. It may take time. You may need to repeat this a few times.

- It is not usually necessary to get up in front of your friends or church and confess publicly.

CONNECTION WITH YOURSELF

To sum it up, we are all made up of body, soul, and spirit, which are all integrated, and each one affects the others. We need to keep a balance in all areas of our life to be in good health.

Taking care of your body is essential. The minute you stop being active and give up on a healthy diet, you begin to slowly decline. Contrary to popular belief, aging does not need to be a bad experience. It can be positive. We don't have to be out of shape and sick as we get older. It is never too late to get back into good health—so long as you are still alive.

Basic health can consist of taking care of your body: there are lots of ways you can take care of yourself. But there is no replacement for exercise and healthy eating.

- Drink a few glasses of water each day. Your body needs to stay hydrated, and water also flushes out toxins that can settle in your organs. I'm not saying how many glasses to drink, just to drink water daily.

- Radically reduce anything you do to your body that is not good or that you do in excess. This might include excessive alcohol use, drugs, smoking, overeating, or foods that are bad for you.

- Find ways to stay active. Get out and move and exercise at least a few times a week, if not daily.

Walking 20 to 30 minutes three to four times a week will do wonders. Find something that works for you and stick with it. Things like using a treadmill, jumping on a rebounder, going to the gym—just do something. If the weather is bad, go to the mall and walk. Get creative. Take the stairs instead of the elevator. If you really have to eat fast food, then get out of your car and walk in instead of using the drive-through.

- Consider the types of foods you eat. Most Americans live on an excessive amount of processed foods that are chemically altered. If you are not willing to reduce or minimize heavily processed food, at least include something besides hamburgers, fries, and microwave dinners. Add some naturally grown substances such as fruits and vegetables and salads to your diet. I am sorry to break the news, but French fries do not qualify as a healthy vegetable.

We have already covered the details of how to improve and care for your emotions and your spiritual life. I will recap some of the points that you will do well and good to remember.

Take care of your emotions: your emotional well-being is important to live a life of fulfillment. Getting rid of things like worry, anger, gossip, unforgiveness, and bitterness will help. Keep a journal and track how you feel. Talk with trusted friends. Avoid or minimize your exposure with people who are emotionally toxic to you.

- Journal your feelings.

- Talk and interact with other people.

- Take time to be with God, yourself, friends, and family.

- If you are angry, hurting, or feel resentful, then seek help.

Take care of your spirit: spiritual health is just as important as physical and emotional. Spend time reading the Bible and other positive books or listening to CDs on a regular basis.

- Keep a spiritual journal and look for ways that God may be speaking to you.

- Spend time worshiping God and getting together with others who do the same.

- Use your spiritual gifts and natural talents and find ways to love people unconditionally.

Seeing yourself as an integrated person will help balance your life. In the next two chapters, we will cover how to live a balanced life and pinpoint some further steps to get into your destiny.

EXERCISE: BODY, SOUL, AND SPIRIT

Think about the power of connections and how everything in your life affects other areas. Let's bring balance to each of these areas of your life.

Improve your body, soul, spirit.

1. What is one thing you can do to help improve your physical body? Get a physical examination; change your diet; exercise; etc.

2. What is one thing you can do to improve your soul (thoughts, emotions, and desires)? Maybe it is to reconcile a broken relationship; forgive someone; buy a journal; take a class; etc.

3. What is one thing you can do to improve your spiritual life? Go to a seminar; read a book; go to a Bible study; etc.

God created the heavens and the earth, and we are all created in God's image (see Gen. 5:1). Since God is creative, we all have a built-in desire to be creative as well. Too often we think creativity is only for artists, musicians, dancers, or designers. We are all creative in different ways. So let's get creative with this exercise.

Quite often, we might be making headway in our life but may not realize it. It is good to celebrate your successes, accomplishments, or the things you are proud of.

1. Create a storyboard of your life using words. Get a pad of small yellow "sticky-notes." Write one word on each page that describes various aspects of who you are, what you feel called to do in life, and things that excite you. These are the things that energize you. Do as many as you can. Now lay them out on a table so you can see them. You can use words such as *excite, awaken, inspire, laugh, energize, visionary, helper,* etc.

2. Choose the top ten that really stand out. Take those and arrange them in order of most important to least. You might want to place them on the table in the shape of an arrow with your number one as the tip. Take a digital photo and place it somewhere you can see it.

3. Write a one-paragraph statement about your life, what you value, or what excites you based on the top ten words you just came up with.

You can go to www.personaldevelopmentgodsway.com to download the exercise so that you can do it on your computer.

ENDNOTE

1. Allison Kitchen, "Forgiveness: A Key to Better Health," *Vibrant Magazine* (January 2001).

Chapter 12

PRINCIPLES OF ACCOMPLISHMENT

No one can fulfill *your* destiny but *you*. Other people can help coach you and be your cheerleader, but you are the one who has to find what it is that God created you to do and be. Positive change happens when you make a decision to do something and take steps to make it reality. Start small, stay consistent, and over time momentum will build. Transformation occurs when you go beyond your own strength of decision making, tap into God's ultimate power and wisdom to renew your thinking and your behavior, and combine this with practicing the art of good choices.

Transformation requires both God's power and your good choices. Most people either try to do it in their own strength and leave God out, or they focus entirely on being spiritual but fail to be proactive. A balance of both is required. Remember, you can design your life and work with God to discover and reach your destiny.

KEEP YOUR EYES ON THE PRIZE

The apostle Paul says,

> *...But one thing I do: Forgetting what is behind and straining toward what is ahead, I press on toward the goal to win the prize for which God has called me heavenward in Christ Jesus* (Philippians 3:13a-14).

As we develop our life of purpose and destiny, it is important to not get sidetracked or give up. You can't drive your car looking in the rearview mirror, and you cannot live your life based on past experiences. You must get focused and know what it is you want to accomplish and create a plan to get there. Your plan will most likely change—God may change it, or you may change it yourself—but taking steps toward it is what counts. This is what will set you apart from millions of people who live life with no clear direction. You will not want to come to the end of your life without fulfilling what you were destined to do.

Keep your focus on the end result because you will be tempted to quit or settle for less along the way. Life is about love and relationships, not goals and accomplishments. I am saying this to keep you in reality so you don't slip into trying to make things happen through your own efforts. We must do it all through God's strength and power. With this in mind, I want to show you how you can design and live your life in such a way that you don't get overly focused on "To Do Lists" and "Goal Setting."

TRIANGULAR FOCUS

I've heard many different analogies of how to stay focused on what you want to accomplish. It is basically a triangle with a base, a center, and a peak. This represents three areas of focus in our lives in which we spend most of our time and energy.

DAILY ACTIVITIES LEVEL

Most people spend the majority of their time staying busy with activities like going to work, church, picking up the kids, going to meetings, taking the kids to soccer, etc. You stay busy all the time, you feel very little fulfillment. I am not saying that these activities are bad, because they do have value. However, this is the lowest level of focus with regard to getting you to your destiny and finding fulfillment in life. Raising your children might be your purpose right now, but if you are only focusing on their activities, then you will need to consider the bigger picture of how to develop them into their future. We all have activities, but if that's all you do it will not bring a sense of life fulfillment if you spend the majority of your time and energy at this level.

WORK AND GOALS LEVEL

This is when you begin to learn some effective tools at managing your time, getting organized, and using a PDA or a To-Do List. You begin to set and achieve goals. Most people's idea of goal setting occurs only once a year with New Year's resolutions. The failure rate of New Year's resolutions is astonishing. As we learned previously, you have to check back in with your goals to see if you are accomplishing them.

Careers, to-do lists, project planning, and goal setting are all great practices, and you need them in your life. But eventually, if you don't have a greater purpose for why you are working so hard, you will lose focus, get tired, and even burn out. That is why people give up on goal-setting and New Year's resolutions.

LIFE PURPOSE LEVEL

The highest level of fulfillment will come through living at the Life Purpose level. It is what brings the most impact and energy. It is the "reason why" that drives all that you do. Life Purpose gives you a reason for your efforts. It helps define what you are working toward and helps you decide how to invest your time and energy. Living a life of Purpose helps us define these things. People living without Purpose are the ones who grumble and complain about the boss, the company, and the government. Instead of doing something to make the world a better place, they just complain.

> *If people can't see what God is doing, they stumble all over themselves; but when they attend to what he reveals, they are most blessed* (Proverbs 29:18 TM).

When you begin to focus your life on what God shows you about your Purpose and Destiny, you will be greatly blessed. Notice the words: "When they attend to—what God reveals—they will be blessed" You have to take proactive steps—not just believe what God says is true. My life completely turned around when I made the jump from living at the Activities/Goals Level to the Purpose Level.

HOW I MADE THE SHIFT TO LIVING A LIFE OF PURPOSE

When I first discovered many of these principles over 20 years ago, I put together a one-, three-, and five-year plan and I was able to accomplish most of what I set out to do with my career, personal life, and ministry.

During that first five years, I realized that some of the goals in my plan were not realistic so I dropped them and I added others. In the process, I realized that I was in the wrong career! I had been in a 9 to 5 desk job in finance, but I was more suited for a mix of creativity, people-interaction, and flexibility with my time. After accomplishing my five-year career goals, I was feeling great. I mentioned earlier that God had spoken to me through a minister on the radio, who said, "...Jesus is your goal" and I heeded those words and began to move toward pursuing full-time ministry. I was about to discover the purpose and destiny of my life. The very thing I was created to do. I had mastered goals and activities, and I was heading toward finding my life purpose in God.

For me it involved leaving my corporate career and pursuing ministry training. In the process I started my own computer networking business so I could have a flexible schedule to do whatever God directed me to do. That was 1994. After praying and getting wisdom and advice from others, I set a new five-year plan:

- Get deeper emotional healing and develop greater character.

- Find the woman God has for me to marry.

- Get practical ministry training.

- Launch a business with the intention of selling it and use the revenue to start a radical new church.

- Reconcile broken relationships in my life.

- Increase my income by 100 percent or more.

- Get out of debt.

Sounds like a lot to accomplish, but even if I was to hit 50 percent of it I would be much better off than where I was. At the time I was living in a one room bachelor's apartment and driving an old car that had just blown the engine.

By 1999 I accomplished all of this and more. It all did not turn out exactly the way I thought. In fact I had not even realized I had accomplished it until a friend and mentor of mine—Brett Johnson, who helped me form this plan—wrote a book called *Convergence*. He contacted me to use my story of how I left my corporate job and moved into ministry. It was then that I realized that this stuff really does work. This leads me to emphasize again that we must periodically review the goals we write to see how we are doing at accomplishing them. I tell you it would not have happened had I not taken steps. I would still be in my corporate job and still feeling like there was something more.

At that time I had written a life purpose statement. It was to "help people come to know and understand God's love, acceptance, and power in their lives." This is what gave me the strength to endure several years of working hard at running a business and fixing computer networks, sometimes all night for days at a time. I wanted to be doing full time ministry, but I knew that I had things to learn first.

I met my wife Linda, and we married in 1995. She introduced me to her pastor, Charlie Brown, and in 1996 he helped me get the practical ministry training I needed. In 1998 we sold our business and went off to start the radical new church in Kent, Ohio. It was so much fun—and a lot of hard work too! We fixed up an old Harley Davidson motorcycle shop into a grunge coffeehouse with a bar-style band as a worship team. We were reaching college students, professors, psychics and witches, and the kids in the town as well as their parents. They were the most invigorating years of my life.

CHALLENGES WILL COME

A year later, during the grand opening of the coffeehouse church, I found out that my family had a rare genetic disease called Huntington's Chorea that is fatal and incurable. It had killed five of my family members in a year—including my mother—all in 1999. The following year I was tested and found out I have the disease. I handed the church off to someone else and left my job as a pastor due to the symptoms of my illness. I knew deep down that God had promised me that I would do even greater things. I had a choice of giving up or trusting what God promised me was true.

It was the greatest challenge of my life. After working so hard for ten years, I arrived only to get sick and have to leave. The good news is that in 2001, God miraculously healed me of all the symptoms of the disease, which according to the medical field is impossible because it is a degenerative disease. I have been feeling great ever since. I nearly got my eyes off the prize, but my life purpose in God is what drove me to hang on. To this day, my DNA still shows that

I should be sick and my miracle cannot be documented but I am moving forward with life just the same. Though my life should be cut short, I am anticipating many more great years ahead of me.

So, I now use my new purpose statement to keep me on track, and everything I do is in line with it. Even writing this book is helping me reach my ultimate destiny and fits in with the purpose for my life. Having a greater life purpose will motivate you to go beyond just getting a job done to tapping into God's unlimited potential for you.

SETTING A NEW STANDARD

What we really need to motivate us is to set a new standard of possibilities. Bill Gates set out to create the best software company in the U.S. He decided early on that his operating system would be on nearly every computer on the planet. His purpose drove him, a young college dropout, to overtake IBM. People thought he was insane, but it worked.

Roger Bannister was the first human to run the mile in less than four minutes. It was considered to be impossible at that time. He broke the record in 1954 and set a new standard for what is possible. Within a short period of time, others were doing the same. We often limit ourselves to our own thinking or understanding. People like Bill Gates and Roger Bannister set new standards for posibilites. We need to remove the limitations:

..with God all things are possible (Matthew 19:26).

According to the standards of medicine, I should be sick and not be doing what I am doing today. Through God's strength I am setting a new standard. I am not boasting—I am laughing, because I was a near high school dropout—I have not attended college outside of a couple of classes years ago. Because I was willing to go for all that God has for me, the books I've written are being used as text books in several Bible colleges. You might say I got a Ph.D. in getting results. But more than that I am living for God's purposes and influencing others to do the same.

Yes, God is the one who strengthens me and gives me the influence and creditability with people. But I also had to say, "Yes, I will do it" and actually follow through and do it. It has to be a combination of both—you and God working hand in hand.

When I was writing my first book, *Prophesy, Dreams and Evangelism*, God spoke to me that He had asked two people prior to me to write it, but apparently they either said no or did not manage their time well enough to do it. That gave me more leverage to get myself to follow through and write the book. God is calling all of us to a higher standard, but few people are answering that call. Most are still waiting for God to do it for them.

CONTINUAL IMPROVEMENT ALWAYS (CIA)

A great deal of research has been done in businesses regarding quality management. Many businesses have experienced a turnaround and have become successful by accepting the idea that there is always room for improvement, even in areas that "aren't broken". Using this philosophy, new possibilities are discovered that might have been previously overlooked. Being open to areas of improvement will help you in your life journey.

Committing yourself to growth and improvement is essential. Like anything in life and nature, if you don't feed it, it will die. You must continually feed and train yourself and exercise your gifts and talents.

Solid food is for those who are mature, who have trained themselves to recognize the difference between right and wrong (Hebrews 5:14 NLT).

Since I had wasted half of my life on drugs, I wanted to get to my destiny as quickly as possible. I made a commitment to self study, mentoring, and practical training. For years I had a corporate job that started at 9 A.M. I got up at 5 A.M. to pray, listen to tapes, and read books, and I spent my lunch hour studying workbooks and correspondence courses. I used my commute time the same way. I did not let up. I combined this with mentoring and internships with organizations that were doing what I wanted to do. I volunteered at ministries to get experience. I was so hungry to learn. I took little steps that at the time did not seem like much, but over a decade those steps made a big difference in my life.

People can go to college and still not know what they want to do. The reason for this is that many people go to college with a goal to "get a degree." So once you reach that goal, you are left feeling like "What's next?" You can reach your goal and get a degree, and still not have a great career. You must set your focus on being the best that you can in all that you do. I believe in higher education, and I could have gone a lot farther early on in my life with it. But applying and putting into action what you learn will take you much farther than gaining knowledge in and of itself. So get a college degree if you feel directed to do so, but be sure to practically apply your knowledge and gain experience at the same time. This is the reason why some people succeed and some do not. Committing yourself to lifelong learning is easy to do, and it only takes a few easy steps each day or week.

STEPS FOR DEVELOPING A CIA LIFESTYLE

- Schedule yourself to go to a training event or conference at least once a year. It could be on anything that will help you to grow; things like personal healing or improvement in your profession. If you do not schedule it, it will not happen. Pray and ask God to direct you to what you should do.

- If you watch a lot of television, then dedicate one night to read, write, or do creative projects instead. I recommend a DVR (Digital Video Recorder), so you can record the television shows you like and watch them on your schedule without having to see all the commercials. You can at least gain back some time. Most cable companies offer DVR for just a few dollars a month. The time you get back in return is well worth the investment.

- Write and journal ideas that you get. If you don't write them down, you *will* forget them. Carry a pad of paper with you during the day to capture your thoughts or ideas. Or text message yourself with your ideas.

- At the end of each week, look back and see what you may have learned or accomplished. Too often we actually are learning, but we fail to track it.

- Make your personal growth a priority. At one point in my life, I did not have enough money in my savings to both get training that I desperately needed and also buy a car I badly needed. So I got creative and bought a good used car for several thousand dollars less and used the extra money for the training. It is all where your priorities are. You can find a way if you really want it and value it.

FAST TRACKING TO YOUR FUTURE

I've been told that it is not a good thing to try to fast track. I do realize that there are some life lessons for maturity that you cannot shortcut around them. You can, however, learn them quickly and reduce the time of going through repeated testing.

One area that you cannot hurry is God's timing and the favor or creditability that He gives you. If you feel God directing you to be in some type of leadership position, you will need to wait for proper recognition from those who are over you. You can help the process along by talking to your leaders and asking them what changes you need to make to grow in maturity. If you intentionally pursue the maturity process, you will get there quicker as opposed to aimlessly waiting for it to happen.

If your church does not have a training track in place to help people get to what they are called to do, then find the training you need either using the Internet or visiting other churches in town. I am not recommending that you leave your church. I used to go to a different church in my town, with my pastor's recommendation, that taught classes on evangelism, which was the area I wanted to grow in. There are lots of Schools of Ministry that specialize in training and equipping. Most of these schools have correspondence courses or training via the Internet available. You cannot bypass maturity, but you can shorten the time of your learning. Simply pursue learning the lessons quickly and apply them to your life. My organization offers several online courses and we do live and recorded webinars. Visit www.dougaddison.com for more information.

FIND SOMEONE WHO IS DOING WHAT YOU WANT TO DO

Assuming you are addressing the issues we have talked about in this book, you can cut down the time it takes to get to what you are called to do. One way is to find someone who is doing what you want to do and study their life, material, and model after their success. The beauty of books is that many people pour a lifetime of knowledge and experience into them, and you can read them in a few days and gain their wisdom without having to go through their pain.

The material in this book has taken me 20 years to live and learn and over 1,500 hours to research and compile. You can go through it and get the benefit of my labor in a fraction of the time. Modeling after someone does not mean to copy everything they do. Simply learn from them and build on their foundation. Most successful people, even those in ministry, did not just wake up one day successful. They made choices and found ways when there seemed to be no way to find.

GET A MENTOR

I hesitate using the term *mentor* since there may be misunderstandings about what it means. A mentor is anyone who is doing some aspect of what you want to do or who has wisdom and advice that will help you get to where you are going. You can mentor with people without even contacting them—or they may be from the past. The first step is to familiarize yourself with their teachings, ethics, and history. If they have books, read everything they have and listen to their audios and begin to formulate an overview of their material. If it is someone you know, then go to coffee or lunch and prepare a list of specific questions to ask them.

The first step to getting a mentor is realizing what real mentoring is all about. Years ago I wanted to use dream interpretation as a means of evangelism to people who are saying that they are "spiritual but not religious." So I found several ministries doing what I wanted to do. I narrowed it down to Streams Ministries International. First I studied all the material thoroughly and took all the courses. I wanted to go even further, and I had questions, so I asked if I could be mentored by this ministry.

Being mentored meant that I had to be the Webmaster and handle all the technical aspects for their ministry because they had no other job openings. Much of what I did was voluntary at first. I had to do set-up for conferences, answer phones, clean bathrooms, and whatever needed to be done. I had very little one-to-one time being mentored, as most people might expect, but I studied and learned and eventually became one of their most successful instructors. Later I went on to launch my own ministry and develop my own training courses.

I CAN BE YOUR MENTOR

People contact me all the time and say they want me to be their mentor. First I want to say that I am honored that anyone would consider this. Because I travel a lot, I actually have very little time to mentor someone one-on-one in the sense that they think mentoring should be. My first question is, have you read my books and taken my seminars, or been part of my webinars? I also offer lots of free downloads and articles on my Web site and my blog. That is the first step. If you have not done this, then I recommend to start there. The more you hear my message, the more mentoring you will receive.

Most of the people I have mentored never asked me directly to mentor them. They began to come to my events and volunteering their time to help with whatever needs to be done. Many of them have taken my leadership classes and now have their own businesses and ministries. I see the value of mentoring, and I offer live Webcasts to accomplish this. We utilize technology and have interactive Internet groups on Facebook.com and on our own Web site.

I recommend getting the input from many different leaders and people. There are people at your work, school, in your church, or community who are treasure chests of knowledge and experience. Utilize them to bounce ideas off of and get wisdom.

It will also help you to help others. You can be a mentor to someone else. If you have learned anything in your life's journey then share it with others. The more you give, the more you will receive.

BUILD A WINNING TEAM AROUND YOU

When you are making changes in your life, you may find that some friends and colleagues you used to spend a lot of time with no longer are on the same page as you are. I am not saying to dump your friends, unless they are toxic for you. I came out of a drug culture and had to get away from my pack of partying animals in order to move toward my destiny. I can now go back around them and be a positive influence.

Begin to recognize people in your life and identify key relationships that are on the same track as you are. Remember "birds of a feather flock together." Find others who are on the same track as you so that you can help each other. Find people you can talk with about all the changes you are going through and your struggles. Chances are, you already know a good number of people who are more than willing to help you out in some way. Remember the A.S.K. principle:

> **Ask** and it will be given to you; **seek** and you will find; **knock** and the door will be opened to you. For everyone who asks receives; he who seeks finds; and to him who knocks, the door will be opened (Matthew 7:7-8).

Here are a few steps to consider. Find or start a peer group: people who are like minded that meet for coffee or have a conference call weekly or at least once a month. Find people who you can contact for good wisdom and advice. Hire a coach, whether spiritual, results-oriented, or to help you with productivity. Join an online community. The Internet is a wonderful but often untapped resource. When I wrote my first book, I joined an online community of writers to bounce questions off of and to get encouragement.

HIRE A COACH

Coaching is a method of helping you create a desire for lasting change in any area of your life. It's a way of helping you achieve your maximum potential and become all that God created you to do and be. In the past, the idea of "hiring a coach" was only thought of in sports. Coaching is now becoming popular in business and personal development organizations.

Most people live their lives with hidden fears and limiting beliefs that stop them from moving forward. They've developed subconscious patterns which prevent them from living the life that they really want.

Coaching helps you to identify these patterns and create new strategies that make it easy to work through obstacles and get results. Coaching usually happens over the telephone two to three times a month for whatever period of time that is needed to help you.

Coaching is very different from counseling.

The difference between coaching and counseling:

COUNSELING	COACHING
Helps sick people	Helps healthy people
Deals with the past	Deals with the future
Sometimes hurts	Feels great
Takes time to see results	Results come relatively fast

I have a group of life purpose coaches who are trained in the material in this book. If you are interested in hiring one of our coaches, you can check my Web site or contact my office.

SMART GOAL SETTING

What is a planning and goal-setting teaching without reiterating the need to set SMART goals and plans? There are many acronyms used for setting goals. My favorite and the most popular for SMART goals is being specific, measurable, attainable, realistic, and time sensitive. SMART goals were made popular by Peter Drucker in 1954 in his book, *The Practice of Management*. This is not to be confused with DUMB Goals which are doable, understandable, manageable, and beneficial. Though DUMB goal setting might work, the name stood in the way from it becoming popular.

Specific—know exactly what it is you want to do.

Measurable—how will you know you are doing it?

Attainable—set yourself up to win; it should be something you can do and get excited about.

Realistic—the sky is the limit, but keep it within what can be done given your current resources. Longer-range goals can be more aggressive.

Time Sensitive—when will you start and when will you finish?

Set yourself up to win and feel good about yourself—keep it realistic—don't underestimate the time it takes to accomplish things. Be sure not to bite off more than you can chew.

CREATING THE MAP (MANAGEABLE ACTION PLAN)

No matter what you want to accomplish, it helps to get clear on what you want to do. When I began the process of researching and writing this book several years ago, I created a MAP, and after listing my steps, I determined it would be more effective to first release it as both a live seminar and a self-study audio course. This would allow me to test my theories and get feedback before writing a book that would go out to a broader audience. I was writing the manuscript for the self-study course in August of 2006 with the goal of having it ready by the end of the year. As I completed my MAP, I realized that it was going to take over a year of very diligent work, as opposed to six months as I had initially intended. The MAP got me into reality. You'll see my sample below.

A Manageable Action Plan is very easy to do. Just follow this pattern:

- Clearly state what you want to accomplish by when.

- Give yourself a good reason why you must do it.

- List your steps and place dates next to each.

- Begin to do something right away—take a step now!

- Check back in each week or month to see what needs changed.

Learn to plan backward whenever you can. Think about how you want to be at the end of your allotted time to complete the MAP. Let's say you want to accomplish something within one year from now. Go out 12 months and work backward. In 12 months I want to have done the following. Within 6 months, 3 months, 1 month (what you want to have accomplished in a month), 1 week (something you can do next week), 1 day (something you can do right now).

This process is also beneficial in planning your week. Think of the end of the week and what are two to three things you would like to accomplish that give you the most impact or satisfaction. Then plan around those items.

SAMPLE MAP TO LOSE WEIGHT

Here's an example of how I used the MAP to lose weight several years ago.

What I want to do:

Lose 20 pounds.

When I want to complete it:

Within 3 months.

Why I must get myself to do this:

If I don't take care of my body, then I will not live long enough or be in good enough health to fulfill my destiny. When I am a great example to others as a Christian, more people will be drawn to God.

Steps to take/Plan backward:

I want to get an exercise plan that I can do at home and in hotel rooms while I travel. Change my diet so that I can have more energy. Get cholesterol checked and get a physical exam.

90 days:

1. Lose 20 pounds.

2. Walking 3 times per week.

3. Buy new clothes because I lost the weight!

30 days:

1. Find exercise program, DVD, or book—March 7.

2. Contact nutritionist for a balanced diet plan—March 21.

3. Decide on diet to go with—March 30.

This week:

1. Go for a walk tomorrow morning.

2. Buy new music for iPod to make walking exciting.

Actions I can take now:

1. Throw out junk food.

2. Make a promise to God and myself to lose 10 pounds.

3. E-mail accountability partner to let them know what I am doing.

4. Find my walking shoes.

Set up a follow-up date to check back in and measure your results.

Check in 30 days <u>March 30</u>

How is it going?

I bought a workout book and have been doing it diligently. I have been exercising daily for 30 days. I lost 5 pounds.

Anything need changed?

I need new walking shoes.

Check in 60 days <u>April 30</u>

How is it going?

I have lost 12 pounds and feel much better.

Anything need changed?

After getting advice, I found that I actually need to lose 25 pounds. I bought heart rate monitor to get my heart pumping on my walks.

Check in 90 days <u>May 30</u>

How is it going?

I have lost 16 pounds!!! Found the right workout exercises to do while traveling. Have been doing them every other day and increasing reps. Got cholesterol checked, and I am OK.

Anything need changed?

Need to get a physical exam. Keep on routine and I should be able to maintain the weight I lost.

There is a sample MAP form in the back of this book. You can also go to my Web site and download one that you can print out and use or make one that best suits your needs. After you get in the habit of breaking through instead of avoiding tasks, this type of planning becomes natural. You can apply this to any area of your life.

This is a great tool for project management. If you fill out a MAP for projects and someone approaches you and asks you if you need help with anything, then you have your action steps clearly defined so you can assign them a subtask. Getting clear about what you want and why, and even a few steps to get there, actually removes the stress. The key is to not allow this type of planning to stress you out. It is not intended to add stress, but to help alleviate it because you are being realistic about what needs to be done.

Speaking of reality, I create MAPs for projects and tasks in my life. I recently found a MAP for a book I was going to finish writing and release over a year. Halfway through I felt God direct me to put it on hold. So I was planning, but God directed my steps.

Be sure to find ways to have fun while you do it. The MAP of my weight loss plan was real. I ended up losing 30 pounds and have maintained it for over seven years. I had challenges along the way. Last year I tried changing my diet and I gained 10 pounds and had a difficult time losing it. It was a blessing in disguise, as I had no idea that my metabolism had flatlined and even though my weight was fine, my immune system was weak. In the process of "checking back," I was able to change my diet so that I am now much healthier than I was before and I eventually got the 10 pounds off again by taking small steps on a regular basis.

I'm just saying, be sure to not get too critical or place a heavy weight of rules on yourself. Live each day to its fullest because today will never be here again.

EXERCISE: CREATE A MAP

1. At what level of the Triangular Focus on page 227 do you spend most of your time and energy?

2. To live with a Life Purpose focus requires finding things you are excited about or feel called to do. Think of something you want to accomplish or do in your life and do some research about it on the Internet or at the library. Write out a SMART Goal about how to accomplish it.

3. Find someone who is doing what you want to do or has written a book on it. Come up with three questions you could ask them that would help you in your journey. Now contact them and ask your questions.

4. Consider getting a mentor or a coach to help you get to your destiny much more quickly.

5. Create a MAP based on a task or decision you have made. Maybe it is a project or something you want to accomplish. Use the MAP form in the back of this book or go to my Web site and download one.

You can go to www.personaldevelopmentgodsway.com to download the exercise so that you can do it on your computer.

Chapter 13

BALANCING YOUR LIFE

If you have done the exercises in this book, you should have a few new clues as to your purpose and destiny. Don't be disappointed if it still is not clear. It unfolds over time. I've tried to give you some tools that will help you not only find your destiny but change your life on a daily basis. Even if you were able to apply one principle that changed your life in some way, then it was not a waste of your time. My prayer is that you were inspired by the possibilities of what you can accomplish through God's unlimited love and power.

THE PLATEAU

Most people get excited when they start something new. After the first three to six weeks, the excitement starts to wear off, and the new thing starts to look more like work. To get better at doing the new thing will require additional lessons and regular practice. Sure enough, in a few months to a year, you will hit another plateau, only at a higher level. Most people give it up because it is painful at that point, so they move on to something else and repeat the same process. This can happen in all areas of life, and you need to expect it.

It is the same for some people in regards to new relationships. They find someone new and there is a lot of excitement and everything is fresh and exciting. Then in a few months the glow wears off, and they start experiencing pain. The things you once adored about the person now get on your nerves. Many people don't recognize that this is actually quite normal, so instead of breaking through this plateau, they break up and go from relationship to relationship trying to experience that "first love feeling." They miss out on the fact that relationships help mature us, and true, deep love is developed over time.

When I began to learn and apply the principles I have been sharing with you, I started making massive changes in my life. Then, a few months later, I was doing some of the things I learned, but I found myself slipping back into my old behaviors. This is common and can be expected. Lasting change will not come without practicing what you learned over and over again. I recommend reading back over sections of this book that spoke to you or motivated you in some way.

Picture yourself standing at the base of a mountain. You climb up with lots of energy to 2,000 feet and arrive at a plateau. Even in mountain climbing you have to stop, rest, and adjust to the new altitude. You start climbing again, but now you are starting from 2,000 feet higher than when you began. Each time you start again, your baseline is higher. You are more mature and are stronger. You learn more about yourself. You will not reach the top of a high mountain in one try. You have to pace yourself, and there are camps along the way to rest and refresh. It is the same in life.

For some reason we tend to think that we should be able to start something new and climb to the top and accomplish it all at once.

This is not usually the case, especially when you start changing habits and conditions that have taken a lifetime to perfect.

To succeed and mature, we need to anticipate that we will hit plateaus. It might take some time, but we can make plans to break through to the next level. I remember getting a new principle or idea, and I would launch out like a madman, bringing radical change to my life. I stuck with most of the commitments I made, like exercising, better diet, etc., but I then I would let go of some of the things I learned about managing my time and emotions. I started to slip back into old patterns of stress and over-work and getting out of focus. I suffered for another six months until frustration and dissatisfaction caused me to pick it back up again and start doing things that motivated me again to change.

I started noticing that every six months or so I needed a "shot in the arm." So I would listen to some motivating audios and reread some books and schedule myself to go to some type of encouraging retreat, seminar, or conference. The process of hitting plateaus in my life went on for a number of years, until I recognized it and started to schedule in advance to anticipate it. I made it routine in my life to do motivating things throughout rather than hitting a plateau and becoming frustrated first. If you do this it will soon become second nature for you will be able to coach yourself out of a down time and help others as well. If you find yourself spinning out, reach out to a friend or coach for help.

STEPS TO DEALING WITH THE PLATEAU:

1. Recognize when it happens to you, so you won't think you are losing interest or be tempted to give up. Begin to pray and ask God to strengthen you and give you a plan to get through it.

2. After going through the exercises in this book, put a reminder in your schedule to either revisit this book or do another one within three months.

3. If you are serious about changing your life, then hire a life purpose or performance coach to help you make a plan and follow through.

4. Listen to audios that motivate you. Save any sermons or audios that motivated or inspired you, and listen to them when you need a boost. Repetition is a key to lasting change. I have listened to some audios 20 times or more. I load them on my iPod, and whenever I have some time waiting in line or while driving, I listen to a section. Heck, I even listen to my own audios sometimes.

5. Remind yourself of who you really are—how God sees you. Be sure to renew your mind on a regular basis from any negative inner-dialog.

6. Don't quit! Revise your plan or strategy if needed, but don't give up on your goal or dream.

7. Read some of the articles on my Web site. Download and listen to some of the free audios I have made available. Participate in one of my Webcasts or come to one of my live events. I am committed to continuing to release updated material that will help you in your life journey.

8. You can hire one of our Life Purpose Coaches that can help with the principles in this book.

WHY I WROTE THIS BOOK

After meeting tens of thousands of Christians a year as a conference speaker, I could not help but notice that many people do not know their destiny or even their spiritual gifts. It was sad to me, and I felt God's nudge to do something about it. Over the years I attended training seminars that were not Christian based because I could not find anything like this through Christian organizations. I do not recommend going to secular motivational seminars if you can help it. Many of them can be dangerously seductive with humanistic theology that can get you away from God's will for your life.

Over the years I have been able to go through some secular training events and weed out a lot of the self-focus and new age theology. God directed me to develop this information so you don't have to do any weeding. I have brought together the biblical principles of change and added the element of a relationship with God and utilizing the power of the Holy Spirit. This is the way these principles were intended to be used.

Some Christians think that what I am doing is bringing New Age thinking into the Church. This is far from the truth. What they don't understand is that we need to bring back the powerful biblical principles that Christians stopped using.

AN ENCOURAGING WORD ABOUT DESTINY

Remember, destiny is like a "connect-the-dots" drawing. You don't always know what it looks like until you start following the dots and taking steps. Each and every experience you have can move you toward—or away from—your destiny, based on how you choose to view and respond to it. That is the power of focus. Even if you fail at a task, if you learned something, it will benefit you.

Your destiny will not always be clear. In my life I was always thinking I found my destiny with each thing I did that gave me passion. But after a few years, God would make it clear to me that, though what I was doing was good, it was to train me for something greater.

The vision we have for ourselves is usually too small. We need to break out of limited thinking and into God's unlimited resources.

My advice to you is to faithfully commit yourself to being the best you can with every door of opportunity that God opens to you. When you fall short, admit it, get up, and keep moving forward. Quitting is not an option. Even though I had to quit a job as a pastor, which had been one of my life dreams, due to illness, the whole time I was not working I was trying to find new ways to fulfill my destiny. Then God opened a huge opportunity to me to influence people worldwide. You might have to quit a task, but don't give up on the bigger picture of your destiny.

Destiny and life purpose are like putting together a puzzle. The more pieces you place together, the clearer the picture becomes. There will be times when you feel like you are searching through piles of big-blue-sky puzzle pieces, trying to find anything that will fit. Other times you make a new discovery or find the right puzzle piece, and suddenly things start to all make sense.

BALANCING YOUR LIFE

You might be wondering how you can do all of these new things and keep a balance in your life. It may seem a little overwhelming at first, as with anything new you learn. For instance, if you start going to the gym to get in shape, then you are not at home as much, and your relationships might need attention. Or if you focus more on your career, then your spiritual life could suffer when you work late or on weekends. As you start investing in seminars and programs to develop your new life, then your finances could start to suffer. The key is to stick with it and make the necessary fine-tuning adjustments along the way. In time, your "new thing" will begin to fit into your life as if it had always been there.

GOD'S POWER VERSUS YOUR OWN STRENGTH

The last thing you will want to do is to strive, that is depending on your own strength to achieve anything. Working diligently and striving are not the same things. You don't have to do everything all at once. This process is not intended to overwhelm you. You just completed a crash course in getting focus and clarity in your life. You now have a basic awareness of where you are and the reality of what it will take to get to where you want to go. Remember that change is a process. God will give you the strength to accomplish what you need.

THE PATH OF LIFE—MAKING THINGS ROLL SMOOTHLY

As you apply the principles in this book, some of the things may seem impossible at first. You might find it difficult at first to get a big picture of where your life is currently, and where you are heading or want to go. You probably will not have the time or energy to keep all the plans going for all the different areas of your life. You'll balance one area of your life, and another area goes out of balance, or something happens that needs your attention. That is quite normal. Let's face it—things will never run 100 percent smoothly.

When you solve a set of problems, there will always be another set of problems as a result of the new plan. The fact is, problems will always be there. How you view them and respond to them is what will change your life. Let's look closer at how to get a handle on all the various areas of your life. Of course the most difficult part of balancing your life is…getting started.

> *Problems will always be there.*
> *How you view them and respond to them*
> *is what will change your life.*

GETTING STARTED

My first attempt at balancing my life began with making a list of things I had been putting off. I then chose several major items and used the Pain and Pleasure principle we discussed earlier to get leverage on myself to accomplish them. I recommend that you give this a try. The biggest feedback I get from people who have worked these principles is from the exercise of doing something you have been putting off. It is amazing how much you can accomplish in such a short period of time. Then momentum kicks in; you start to have fun and begin to feel, and even look, better. If you apply these principles regularly, you will have a lifestyle of breakthrough.

PINPOINTING MAJOR AREAS OF LIFE

Most people have two major areas that they need to manage: their professional life and their personal life. Professional does not necessarily mean you have a paid job. It is what you do with the majority of your time. Your profession could be stay-at-home parent, student, or whatever you may be doing in your retirement. For discussion purposes, we'll identify several main categories of the average person's life. I've found that there are six basic categories. Yours may vary.

SIX TOP LIFE CATEGORIES

- *Physical Body*—diet, exercise, staying healthy

- *Emotional Wellbeing*—personal growth, managing your emotions

- *Spiritual Growth*—your gifts, ministry, growth and maturity, relationship with God

- *Financial*—money and debt, giving, investing, saving, planning

- *Career*—or whatever you do with the majority of your time

- *Relationships*—marriage, family, and friends

THE PATHWAY OF LIFE

You can use the graph provided or take a piece of paper and draw your own. Turn the paper horizontally. Draw a straight line across the bottom and one across the top. Divide the page into six even columns and label each column with one of the categories. Now on the far left side, starting at the bottom going to the top, label 0 percent to 100 percent, in 10 percent increments. You will have what looks similar to a graph.

PATHWAY OF LIFE

- Take a moment to think about how satisfied you currently are in each of these areas of your life. Don't think about where you want to be, but think honestly about where you are right now.

Personal Development **God's Way**

	0%	10%	20%	30%	40%	50%	60%	70%	80%	90%	100%
Physical Body											
Emotional Wellbeing											
Spiritual Growth											
Financial											
Career											
Relationships											

- The bottom of the graph is 0 percent and the top is 100 percent. Place a dot in each column that represents your current condition or satisfaction level. In the area of Physical Body, if you are 50 percent satisfied, then place the dot halfway.

- Next step is to connect the dots so that you have a chart of your current condition. Connect Physical to Emotional, and Emotional to Spiritual, etc.

- Now look at the results. Think of this chart as your path of life. Do you have a lot of ups and downs, or is everything rather smooth? Are most of your categories in the low level, or are they high? Is your life running smoothly based on where you are right now? You'll feel better to know that most people have a pretty uneven path. I do this exercise at least once a year and save my results to chart my progress.

DEVELOPING YOUR LIFE PURPOSE

Your life on earth is about accomplishing what you feel destined by God to do and, in the process, becoming more like Christ in nature. If you don't know your purpose or destiny in life, the exercises you have been doing in this program will at least give you some insight into things that motivate you. The things that excite you and give you passion are clues that can help you in your discovery process.

FORMULATE A PURPOSE STATEMENT FOR YOUR LIFE

I don't like using the words *mission statement* because it causes us to get all formal and businesslike. Your *purpose statement* is what you really are all about and comes from your heart. It is in your own words and reflects what you are passionate about.

YOUR LIFE PURPOSE STATEMENT MUST...

- be stated in the positive: I am..., or I will....

- be very brief.

- use your own language, but spice it up.

- be achievable, something you can experience daily.

- be upbeat and exciting.

Example: Doug's Life Purpose Statement

To be a light and guide to millions of people, helping them to transform and discover God's acceptance, love, and power. To have fun, laugh, and grow in all that I do.

Notice in my statement I am helping others and myself. You may need to write a few different statements, then pick one that fits you best.

Get a piece of paper or use your computer and go to a quiet place. Ask God to speak to you, put on some music or whatever allows you to feel creative.

Say these words out loud: "My life purpose is..." and write down whatever comes to you. Do this over and over, writing down every idea and thought. Fill up the page if possible. Don't think it through, but allow it to flow from within you. You don't have to do everything you write down on the paper. You will edit it later. Just let as many statements about your life flow from you as you can.

Next step is to pray over the list and highlight at least three that stand out to you. Using this list, write out a life purpose statement. When you first write it, it will probably be quite long. You will want to get it down to a short paragraph or two to three sentences because you will want to memorize it.

My Life Purpose is:

_____

_____

_____

_____

_____

_____

CREATING A MAP FOR YOUR LIFE

If you were to design plans for all the major areas of your life, it would be a bit overwhelming at this point—unless you are an over-achiever. To keep it simple and help you get started, I want you to identify two areas of your life that you want to create a MAP to accomplish or improve over the next year.

Look at the Pathway of Life chart you just completed. What two areas of your life do you want to work on over the next six months to a year? Think about it and pray about it—don't put it off—do it now. If you pray in more detail later and find you really need to work on another category, it is no big deal to change it.

In the back of this book you will find a MAP form that you can fill out for each of these two areas. Or go to my Web site and download the form to print out or use on your computer. Use a separate form for each life category. You can go to my Web site and download a MAP if you need one. Each year I choose another life category to work on. Sometimes it is my career, my finances, or my relationships. It will change depending on your life situation and season.

IN CLOSING

Commit to walking your talk. Go beyond just believing that it is good for you. Go beyond knowledge, and help others around you change by becoming a living example of how to do it. I want to thank you personally for allowing me to work with you through this book. It is a privilege and a gift to know that I may have helped you in any way, big or small.

If this book has helped you, will you let me know? You can go to my Web site and fill out a feedback form and tell us how it is going for you. If this book has helped you then maybe it will help someone else. Share it with others. Remember, this is not the end; it is the beginning of an entirely new journey. Life is a gift. Love is a gift. Be a giver of life and love by applying what you have learned and to help others.

God's richest blessings on your journey!

EXERCISE: BALANCING YOUR LIFE

I hope you have done all the exercises in the book. They will help you gain some clues about your life purpose and destiny. Go back through the book and finish any exercises that you did not get to.

1. Make a plan now to prepare for hitting a plateau in your progress. Go get your calendar and schedule something for 2-3 months from now. Write down something like "destiny follow up." You don't have to know what it is just yet. It could be that you review these exercises, take a class, read a book, or something practical.

2. Complete the Pathway to Life exercise. Chose two categories that you want to work on over the next six months.

3. Write your Life Purpose Statement. Take the time to do this, as it will help keep you on track later. It will morph and change over time, but getting started on it will really help you.

4. Create a Life MAP for the two categories that you chose from your Pathway to Life. Use the tools and strategies that you have learned from this book to get yourself to follow through and do them. Be sure to check back in 30 and 60 days to see what is working and if you need to make any changes.

Go to my Web site www.personaldevelopmentgodsway.com and look at the additional training that I offer. We have online classes, audios, books, and Life Purpose coaching. Most of all, be sure to enjoy each day of this gift we call life!

MAP—MANAGEABLE ACTION PLAN

Date: _____

Category of life: _____

My Life Purpose Statement: _____

_____

What I want to accomplish: _____

_____

Why I must do it: _____

_____

Plan to get there: List initial steps:

90 days: _____

_____

30 days: _____

_____

Actions I can take now: _____

_____

Set up a follow-up date to check in and measure your results:

Check in 30 days _____ *(fill in date)*

How is it going?

Anything need changed?

Check in 60 days _____

How is it going?

Anything need changed?

Check in 90 days _____

How is it going?

Anything need changed?

MAP—MANAGEABLE ACTION PLAN

Date: _____

Category of life: _____

My Life Purpose Statement: _____

_____

What I want to accomplish: _____

_____

Why I must do it: _____

_____

Plan to get there: List initial steps:

90 days: _____

_____

30 days: _____

_____

Actions I can take now: _____

_____

Set up a follow-up date to check in and measure your results:

Check in 30 days _____ *(fill in date)*

   How is it going?

   Anything need changed?

Check in 60 days _____

   How is it going?

   Anything need changed?

Check in 90 days _____

   How is it going?

   Anything need changed?

MAP—MANAGEABLE ACTION PLAN

Date: _____

Category of life: _____

My Life Purpose Statement: _____

_____

What I want to accomplish: _____

_____

Why I must do it: _____

_____

Plan to get there: List initial steps:

90 days: _____

_____

30 days: _____

_____

Actions I can take now: _____

_____

Set up a follow-up date to check in and measure your results:

Check in 30 days _____ *(fill in date)*

How is it going?

Anything need changed?

Check in 60 days _____

How is it going?

Anything need changed?

Check in 90 days _____

How is it going?

Anything need changed?

AUTHOR MINISTRY PAGE

This book's Web site contains an online community that will allow you to interact with others. You can download and print out the exercises and find additional resources.

www.personaldevelopmentgodsway.com

The author's Web site contains information about Doug Addison's speaking schedule and additional training courses.

www.dougaddison.com

BOOKS BY DOUG ADDISON

Prophecy, Dreams, and Evangelism

Prophecy, Dreams, and Evangelism Study Guide

No More Christianese

Divine Alliances

TRAINING COURSES BY DOUG ADDISON

Accelerating into Your Life's Purpose

Prophetic Evangelism Workshop

Understanding Dreams Workshop

Hearing God Workshop

Kingdom Financial Strategies

Additional copies of this book and other
book titles from DESTINY IMAGE are
available at your local bookstore.

Call toll-free: 1-800-722-6774.

Send a request for a catalog to:

Destiny Image® Publishers, Inc.

P.O. Box 310
Shippensburg, PA 17257-0310

*"Speaking to the Purposes of God for This
Generation and for the Generations to Come."*

**For a complete list of our titles,
visit us at www.destinyimage.com.**